PRENTICE HALL Science Explorer

Inquiry Skills
Activity Book I

PEARSON

Prentice
Hall

Boston, Massachusetts
Upper Saddle River, New Jersey

Note to Teachers

This book is designed to give you the greatest flexibility in teaching, reinforcing, and assessing science skills.

Useful at any time of the year

You can teach these skills lessons at the beginning of the year or as the course progresses. Students do not need to know formal science concepts or scientific terminology to carry out these activities.

No lab equipment required

All activities are "minds-on." Some simple tools such as rulers, protractors, and compasses are needed for certain skills. Graph paper is required for some activities.

Flexible class management

These skills lessons can be used with the whole class, for small group work, or by individuals. Students could begin working individually in class or at home, then discuss their strategies and results in small groups or as a class.

Also see additional notes on specific topics in the Answer Key.

ISBN 0-13-190163-X

6 7 8 9 10 10 09 08

CONTENTS

Basic Process Skills

Designing Experiments

Data Tables and Graphs

Skills Assessment

Answer Key

Name _____ Date _____ Class _____

SKILLS INTRODUCTION

Observing

The first day of school is an exciting time. You find out who your teachers are, who else is in your classes, and where your classrooms are. When you look around to see what the room looks like and who is there, you are making observations.

Observing is using one or more of your senses—sight, hearing, smell, taste, and touch—to gather information about the world. For example, seeing a green chalkboard, hearing a bell ring, smelling smoke, tasting a sour lemon, and feeling a smooth desktop are observations. Information gathered from observations is called evidence, or data. Making and recording observations is the most basic skill in science.

When you make observations in science, you want them to be accurate and objective. An accurate observation is an exact report of what your senses tell you. An objective observation avoids opinions, or bias, based on specific points of view.

Example 1: Sixteen students were present for roll call, and five other students arrived afterward. (accurate and objective)

Example 2: Half the class was late. (not accurate)

Example 3: The friendliest people were there first. (not objective)

Observations can be either qualitative or quantitative. Qualitative observations are descriptions that do not use numbers. For example, if you report colors, smells, tastes, textures, or sounds, you are making qualitative observations. Quantitative observations, on the other hand, do include numbers. If you count objects or measure them with standard units, you are making quantitative observations. Quantitative observations are often made using tools.

Example 4: The classroom walls are yellow. (qualitative)

Example 5: The classroom floor is shiny. (qualitative)

Example 6: There are 21 students in the room. (quantitative)

Example 7: The chalkboard is 1 meter high and 2 meters wide. (quantitative)

Observing *(continued)*

In science, observations are usually followed by attempted explanations, or inferences. When scientists make inferences from observations, however, they keep the two processes separate. That's because although an accurate observation is considered to be factual evidence, the inferences may not be correct. When you make and record your observations, write down just what your senses perceive.

> **Example 8:** There's an empty aquarium tank in the classroom. (observation)
>
> **Example 9:** The tank is 50 cm long, 30 cm wide, and 18 cm deep. (observation)
>
> **Example 10:** The tank used to contain live fish. (an inference, not an observation)
>
> **Example 11:** The tank is waterproof. (an inference, not an observation)

 ## Tips for Making Observations

◆ Use the senses of sight, hearing, touch, and smell to make qualitative observations. Important: For safety's sake, do not taste any unknown substances.

◆ Review your observations to make sure they are accurate and objective.

◆ Whenever possible, count or use instruments to make quantitative observations. Make sure you include the unit that identifies each measurement, such as a mass measurement of 5 grams or a distance measurement of 15 meters.

◆ If no tools are available to make measurements, try to estimate common quantities by referring to known standards. For example, you might state that an object is about as long as a new pencil or has the mass of a paper clip.

◆ Check your observations to be sure that they are statements about information gained through your senses, not explanations of what you observed.

 Write three observations you have made today. Label each observation as qualitative or quantitative.

Name _____ Date _____ Class _____

Observing

Use the illustration to answer the questions that follow. Write your answers on a separate sheet of paper.

1. Make and record at least five qualitative observations of the scene in the illustration.

2. Explain how you could make at least three quantitative observations if you were able to visit this scene.

3. Examine the observations you wrote for Questions 1 and 2. Are any of them actually explanations, or inferences? If so, which one(s)?

4. Is the following statement an observation or an inference? "The house collapsed at the same time that the poles fell down." Explain.

5. Is the following statement an observation or an inference? "The road damage is serious, and it will be very expensive to repair." Explain.

6. Is the following statement an observation or an inference? "The house is built on unstable land." Explain.

7. Is the following statement an observation or an inference? "The damage at this scene was caused by an explosion." Explain.

8. **Think About It** Write a few sentences that would explain to classmates how to keep their observations separate from their inferences.

SKILLS INTRODUCTION

Inferring

Have you ever come home, smelled fish cooking, and thought, "We're having fish for dinner"? You made an observation using your sense of smell and used past experience to conclude what your next meal would be. Such a conclusion is called an inference.

Making an inference, or **inferring,** is explaining or interpreting an observation or statement. Inferences can be reasonable (logical) or unreasonable. A reasonable inference is one that makes sense, given what a person knows about the topic. One way to make an unreasonable inference is to conclude too much from the evidence.

For example, suppose you are on a photo safari in Africa. In a region bordering some small farms, you see some domestic cattle sharing space with some wild antelope. Some people in your group make the following observations and inferences.

Observation: The cattle and the antelope are standing quietly together.

Inference 1: The cattle and antelope do not attack each other. (reasonable)

Inference 2: None of the animals in this region attack each other.
  (unreasonable, because you have no evidence about any other animals)

Observation: Some of the cattle are eating grass.

Inference 3: The grass is food for the cattle and antelope. (reasonable)

Inference 4: Most of the grass in this area is eaten by the cattle. (unreasonable,
  because you have no evidence about the amounts eaten)

Inquiry Skills Activity Book I

Inferring *(continued)*

Often you can make more than one logical inference from the same observation. Remember: A logical inference must make sense in terms of everything else you know.

Observation: The antelope are looking around.

Inference 5: The antelope are watching for predators. (reasonable)

Inference 6: The antelope are watching for potential mates. (reasonable)

Inference 7: The antelope heard you coming through the brush. (reasonable)

When you first make a logical inference, you may not know whether it's true or false. What's important is to make sure the inference is reasonable and based on accurate evidence. Then you can obtain additional evidence to find out whether the inference is correct. For example, if you talked to the farmers who own the cattle in the illustration, you would find out that the cattle eat grass, but the antelope do not.

 ## Tips for Making an Inference

◆ Base your inference on accurate qualitative or quantitative observations.

◆ Combine your observations with knowledge or experience to make an inference.

◆ Try to make more than one logical inference from the same observation.

◆ Evaluate the inferences. Decide what new information you need to show whether your inferences are true. If necessary, gather more information.

◆ Be prepared to modify, reject, or revise your inferences.

 Write at least one additional observation from the illustration on page 8. Then write at least one logical inference you can make from that observation.

SKILLS PRACTICE

Inferring

The diagram below shows the skulls of nine different mammals. (The skulls are not drawn to scale.) Observe the diagram and then answer the questions that follow. Write your answers on a separate sheet of paper.

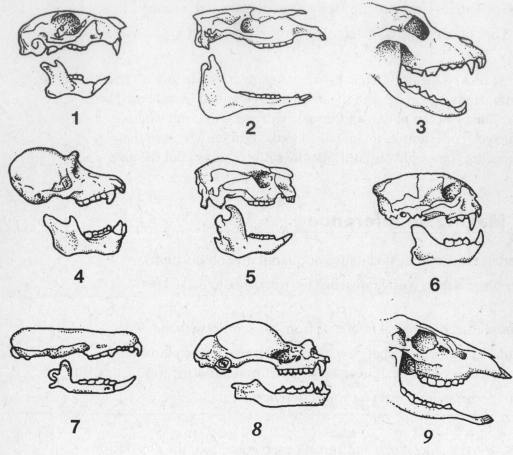

Not drawn to scale

1. A mammal's teeth are adapted to its diet. Some mammals eat only plants. Many of their teeth have flat surfaces that enable the animals to crush and grind the tough material in plant parts. Which of the animals in the diagram have numerous flat teeth? What can you infer about their diet?

2. Some mammals eat other animals. Many of their teeth have sharp points that pierce animal flesh and tear off sections to swallow. Which of the animals in the diagram have numerous sharp teeth? What can you infer about their diet?

3. Some mammals eat both animals and plants. What inference can you make about their teeth? Which animals in the diagram do you think eat both animals and plants?

Inferring *(continued)*

4. You can make other inferences from the skulls of mammals. Look for shadowy indentations and bone shapes that indicate the position and size of the eyes. Which mammals appear to have eyes side by side at the front of the head? Which mammals appear to have eyes on the sides of the head?

5. Mammals that capture other animals for food often have eyes at the front of the head. This position allows them to have excellent depth vision. Mammals that are hunted as food often have eyes on the sides of the head. These animals do not have depth vision, but they can see a larger area around them. Make inferences about the advantages and disadvantages that each type of vision might provide.

6. Which of the mammals in the diagram seems to have very small or no eyes? What might you infer about the mammal(s) based on these eyes?

7. Based on the animals' teeth and eyes, which one of these mammals, if any, might hunt other animals for food?

8. Based on the animals' teeth and eyes, which one of these mammals, if any, might eat only plant materials?

9. Based on the animals' teeth and eyes, which one of these mammals, if any, might eat both animals and plants?

10. **Think About It** Scientists sometimes find skulls or parts of skulls from extinct animals, ones that are no longer found alive anywhere on Earth. How might they use inferences to learn about these animals from past times?

SKILLS INTRODUCTION

Predicting

If a family moves into your neighborhood, your new neighbors may ask you questions like these: How many games will the school soccer team win? Will the math teacher give hard quizzes? How long will it take to get to the library? Questions like these ask you to make predictions. Predictions are a normal part of everyday life, but they also have an important place in science.

Predicting is making an inference about a future event based on current evidence or past experience. One way to make a prediction is to look for a pattern. For instance, depending on how many games your soccer team won last year, and whether the same players are on the team, you might make one of the predictions below. Notice that these predictions differ in how specific they are.

> **Example 1:** Our team will lose a lot of games this year.
> (general)

> **Example 2:** Our team will win about half of its games this year.
> (somewhat specific)

> **Example 3:** Our team will win at least six games, but it will lose to
> Central Community School. (quite specific)

When you make a prediction in science, try to make it as specific as you can. Don't just guess. Consider all the experiences and knowledge you have about the topic. Also examine any new information you can obtain, by analyzing data tables and graphs, for example. Then make a reasonable inference based on all that information.

You may have made a logical prediction that did not come true. As a result, you probably know that predictions are not always correct. Because a prediction is an inference—an explanation or an interpretation of observations—it may not turn out to be true.

In science, predictions are usually tested. Some predictions can be tested by making observations. For instance, if someone predicts the times for sunrise and sunset over the next 30 days, you can test those predictions by using an accurate watch to time the events each day. On other occasions, carefully planned tests may be needed. For instance, suppose someone makes this prediction:

> "This new medicine will prevent the common cold."

The only way to test such a statement would be to carry out a controlled experiment. Regardless of whether tests show a scientific prediction to be true or false, making and testing predictions is a proven way of increasing people's understanding of the natural world.

Predicting *(continued)*

▷ Tips for Making Predictions

◆ When you make a prediction about an event, don't just guess. Examine all the evidence that's available to you, including information in data tables and graphs. Also recall what you know about the topic.

◆ Look for a pattern in the evidence or in what you know. Consider how that pattern applies to the event you're predicting.

◆ If you don't have enough information, try to find out more about the event or about similar events.

◆ Don't be discouraged if your prediction turns out to be false. Remember that the purpose of making a prediction in science is to learn about the natural world. Always ask yourself, "What did I learn from making and testing this prediction?" Your early incorrect predictions may lead you to new questions and new predictions that will increase your knowledge.

 **Reading Checkpoint**   Explain why making a prediction in science is different from just guessing.

SKILLS PRACTICE

Predicting

Suppose you and your friend find a box filled with samples of different solid materials. All the samples come in cubes, and the cubes are all of the same size—1 cm on each side. (A cube is a solid figure having six square sides that are equal in size.)

You drop nine of the sample materials into a bucket of water. You observe that some cubes float. Some others sink. Using your observations and the information that comes with the samples, you make a data table that looks like this.

Table 1: Sinking/Floating Test Results		
Sample Material	Mass of Cube	Observed Results
Apple tree wood	0.84 g	Floated
Asphalt	1.5 g	Sank
Beeswax	0.96 g	Floated
Brick	1.4 g	Sank
Cement	2.7 g	Sank
Cork	0.22 g	Floated
Granite	2.64 g	Sank
Marble	2.84 g	Sank
Paraffin	0.91 g	Floated

Your friend brags that she can predict which of the remaining cubes will sink and which will float. You challenge your friend that you can get more predictions right than she can. You make a data table like the one at the right for the remaining samples.

TABLE 2: Sinking/Floating Test Predictions		
Sample Material	Mass of Cube	Predicted Results
Anorthite	2.74 g	
Balsa wood	0.14 g	
Charcoal	0.57 g	
Coal	1.4 g	
Diamond	3.52 g	
Dolomite	2.84 g	
Ebony wood	1.33 g	
Glass	2.4 g	
Peat	0.84 g	
Tar	1.02 g	
Sealing wax	1.8 g	

Predicting *(continued)*

Answer the following questions on a separate sheet of paper.

1. One way to predict which materials will float or sink is to use your knowledge and past experience. Make as many predictions as you can about the materials listed in Table 2 on page 14. Give your reason for each prediction.

2. Examine the information provided in Table 1 on page 14. Try to find a pattern indicating why some cubes floated and some sank. Write down any pattern you find. (*Hint:* You could make two new data tables, listing the materials that floated in one table and the materials that sank in the other table.)

3. Use the pattern you found in Question 2 to predict which of the remaining sample materials will float and which will sink.

4. Do any of your predictions from Question 3 contradict your predictions from Question 1? If so, which one(s)? Which of the two different predictions do you now think is right? Explain.

5. **Think About It** You have probably observed that ice cubes float in water. Write a prediction stating the mass of an ice cube 1 cm on each side. Explain your prediction.

Name _____ Date _____ Class _____

Classifying

Can you imagine shopping for a CD in a store that kept its recordings in a single, huge pile? Chances are you'd take your business to a place that classified CDs into groups, such as rock, rap, country, and other categories.

Classifying is organizing objects and events into groups according to a system, or organizing idea. The most simple type of classification system uses two groups, one that has a certain property and another that does not. Other systems may begin with three or more groups.

Example 1: Plants With Wood; Plants Without Wood (simplest system using two groups)

Example 2: Locations at Sea Level, Locations Above Sea Level; Locations Below Sea Level (three groups based on one idea)

Many classification systems, like the one in the diagram above, have more than one level. Each of the first-level groups in the system is further classified into smaller categories based on new organizing ideas.

In science, objects and processes can be classified in different ways. Scientists choose the system that best suits their purpose. They may classify to organize objects, such as the chemicals stored in a laboratory. They also classify to help simplify and make sense of the natural world. Good classification systems make finding information easier. They also help to clarify the relationships among the things being classified.

▶ Tips for Classifying

◆ Carefully observe the group of objects to be classified. Identify similarities and differences among the objects.

◆ Choose a characteristic that some of the objects share. Using this characteristic as the organizing idea, place the objects into groups.

◆ Examine the groups and decide if they can be further classified. Each round of further classification may need a different organizing idea.

 Reading Checkpoint   Develop a classification system for your clothes that has at least two levels. Write a word or phrase that shows the organizing idea for each grouping.

SKILLS PRACTICE

Classifying

The 8 rows of illustrations that follow contain 32 animals. (The illustrations are not drawn to scale.) There are many different ways to classify these animals. As you try out various organizing ideas, don't be discouraged if you have to revise some of those ideas.

Use the illustrations to answer the questions on page 19.

1.

Alligator

Bluebird

Chicken

Cow

2.

Deer

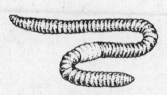
Duck

Earthworm

Eel

3.

Elephant

Fly

Frog

Goose

Classifying *(continued)*

4.

| Grasshopper | Guppy | Hawk | Jellyfish |

5.

| Lizard | Monkey | Octopus | Ostrich |

6.

| Pig | Ray | Robin | Salamander |

7.

| Salmon | Seal | Shark | Sheep |

8.

| Tiger | Tortoise | Tuna | Turtle |

Classifying *(continued)*

Use the illustrations on pages 17 and 18 to answer the following questions. Write your answers on a separate sheet of paper.

1. Develop a classification system for the animals that contains just 2 groups. Give a name to each group, and classify the animals according to this system.

2. Develop a classification system for the animals that uses 3–5 groups. Give a name to each group, and classify the animals according to this system.

3 Develop a classification system for the animals that contains 2 levels. You can use one of your systems from Questions 1 and 2, or develop a new system. Use a diagram to show all the groups in your system.

4. Classify the animals according to the system that you developed in Question 3. (*Hint:* You may want to use a data table to organize your lists.)

5. Suppose that you are designing a zoo. Your goal is to prepare exhibits that will be easy to maintain. Would you use any of your classification systems from Questions 1–4 to plan the zoo? Explain.

6. **Think About It** Which of the classification systems that you developed in Questions 1–4 would help you learn the most new information about animals? Explain.

Name _____ Date _____ Class _____

Making Models

You may know someone who builds model trains, ships, or dollhouses as a hobby. In some occupations, people use models to plan complex objects, such as buildings. Models also play a role in science. Scientific **models** are pictures, diagrams, or other representations of objects or processes. Models may be created on paper or on a computer, or may be made of wood, metal, plastic, or other materials. Making scientific models helps people understand natural objects and processes.

There are two main types of models. Physical models, such as model skeletons, usually look like the object or process being modeled. Mental models, such as mathematical equations, represent ideas about objects or processes that often cannot be directly observed. For example, for centuries, most people thought that the world was flat. A few scientists developed the hypothesis that Earth is shaped like a ball. They could then make a mathematical model that included the diameter of Earth and use an equation to find Earth's surface area.

Physical models can be either two-dimensional (flat), such as a map, or three-dimensional (with depth), such as a globe. Scientists often use physical models to represent things that are very large (such as the solar system), very small (atoms), or not easily visible (bacteria). Some models are drawn "to scale." That means that the measurements of the model are in proportion to the actual object. For example, a model may be 100 times larger than or $\frac{1}{10}$ the size of the actual object.

Tips for Making Models

◆ Identify the purpose of the model and the type of model to be used (physical or mental, two-dimensional or three-dimensional).

◆ If you are modeling a process, try to think through the entire process and identify its steps in order.

◆ If you are making a physical model, determine what materials you will use.

◆ Decide whether the model will be larger than, smaller than, or the same size as the real object. Will it be made to scale? If so, what scale?

◆ Make a plan before you begin making the model. Use pencil to list or draw your ideas, and have an eraser handy so you can revise your plan easily. Be prepared to explain any important differences between the model and the real thing.

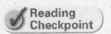
Reading Checkpoint What do scientific models have in common with models people make for enjoyment? How are the two kinds of models different?

Name _____ Date _____ Class _____

Making Models

Use a separate sheet of graph paper to make each of the two models described below. To obtain the measurements you need, use a meter stick or make estimates. Then answer the following questions on a separate sheet of paper.

Suppose that your school principal is considering changing the way your classroom is arranged. To help in the planning, you are asked to (1) make a two-dimensional scale model of your classroom as it is; (2) make a similar model to show how the classroom might be rearranged; (3) explain whether or not your new arrangement is an improvement over the current arrangement.

1. Read over the rest of the assignment. Make a plan of your tasks, such as taking certain measurements or listing objects that will appear in your model. Decide whether you will use a meter stick to obtain actual measurements of objects and distances, or if you will estimate those measurements.

2. Measure or estimate the size of your classroom floor. What are the room's length and width?

3. What scale will you use to draw the floor? (*Hint:* Decide how many squares on your graph paper will represent the length of your classroom. For example, if the room is 18 meters long, you could use a scale in which the length of 1 square represents 1 meter.) Find a place on the graph paper to describe your scale, and write in that scale.

4. Draw the length and width of the classroom floor to scale on the graph paper. Using the same scale, draw the major structures around the edge of the room, such as doors, closets, and bookshelves. Label these structures.

5. Using the same scale, draw in the main pieces of furniture within the classroom, such as the teacher's and students' desks and chairs and any other items you think are important. Label these objects.

6. Use a new sheet of graph paper to make a new model showing a different classroom arrangement. Keep the floor the same size and show the same number of desks and chairs. Show the location of all structures that appear in your first model. (*Hint:* Remember to label all structures and objects.)

7. Use your models to decide which classroom arrangement works better. Be sure to consider such needs as making quick exits during fire drills and giving all students access to the bookshelves. Explain which version you prefer, and give your reasons.

8. **Think About It** Do you think a physical model has to show every part of the object or process being modeled? Use the models you just made to help explain your response.

Name _____ Date _____ Class _____

Making Models *(continued)*

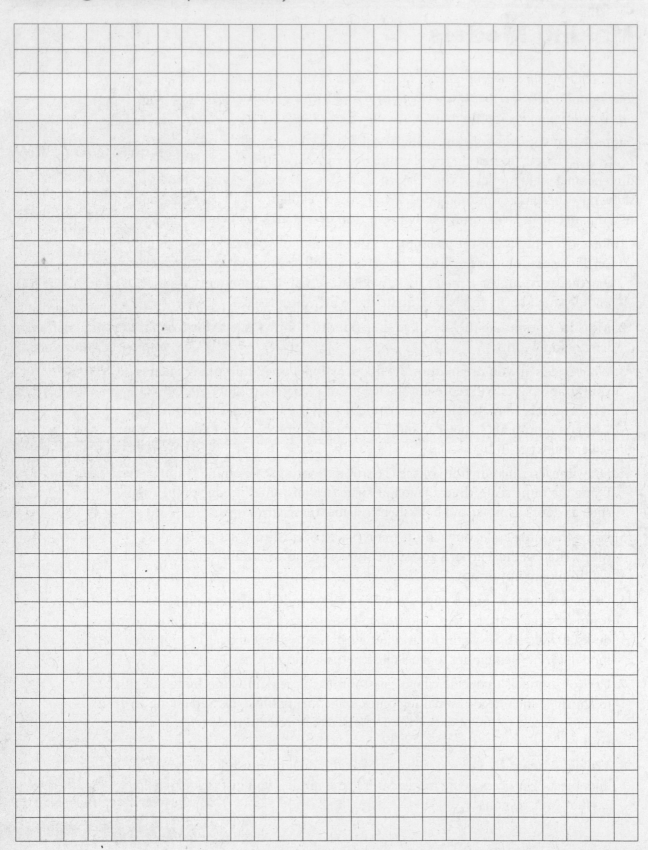

Name _____ Date _____ Class _____

Communicating

You have probably waved to a friend from a distance, written someone a note, and had more conversations than you can count. Whenever you send messages to, or receive messages from, another person, you are **communicating.** Since you've been communicating your whole life, you may wonder what else you need to learn about the topic.

Now you are learning how scientists communicate. In science, observations and experiments should be reproducible. That means that any scientist should understand and be able to repeat the work of another scientist. To make such repetition possible, scientists follow certain rules when they communicate.

◆ The descriptions of all procedures must be understandable and complete. Someone else should be able to to repeat the entire procedure step by step.

◆ Observations, or evidence, must be recorded accurately and in total. Researchers who observe unexpected or puzzling results must report these results.

◆ The observations should be discussed separately from the inferences, or explanations of the observations. Other scientists may make different inferences from the same observations.

◆ Scientific work should be objective—free from bias. In science, being free from bias means considering all reasonable explanations instead of just trying to prove a specific idea.

As you study science, you'll have many opportunities to communicate, sometimes orally and other times in writing.

Oral Communication Scientific communication may occur orally. Scientists frequently share their ideas in person and by telephone. You too will have opportunities to talk about science topics when you work in small groups or make presentations to your class. Besides observing the rules described in the previous section, try to remember the following:

◆ Your ideas may be new to your audience. Watch people's faces to see if they understand you. You may need to repeat an idea or explain it in a different way.

◆ Consider using visuals or models. In small groups, you could make simple sketches. For class presentations, you could prepare larger, more complex displays.

Communication *(continued)*

Written Communication Most scientific communication occurs through the written or printed word. New research is nearly always reported in printed form, usually in science journals. Similarly, you may need to write up the procedures and results of your experiments in a lab report. Lab reports usually contain the following sections, in this order:

(1) problem or question

(2) hypothesis

(3) list of materials

(4) procedure

(5) observations, often organized in data tables

(6) analysis, including any calculations and graphs

(7) conclusions

Sometimes lab reports end with additional questions suggested by the conclusion or ideas for additional experiments.

Tips for Communicating in Science

◆ Describe your observations honestly and completely. Write what you actually observe, not what you expected to observe or hoped would happen.

◆ Record your observations as clearly and efficiently as possible, for example, using data tables. If you make data tables afterward, always create those data tables from your original notes. Don't rewrite your notes to make them sound better.

◆ Keep a written record of your procedures, including any changes you make as you work. Always be prepared to communicate your procedures to others.

◆ Present your observations and your inferences separately.

◆ Use graphs and diagrams when they will help interpret your data. If you carry out calculations, show the formula or describe the mathematical operations you performed.

◆ Follow any rules or guidelines that apply to the specific type of communication, for example, lab reports, science fair presentations, and class projects.

◆ If you use information from other people's work, keep a record of those references and the information you obtained from them. Be prepared to provide the names of your sources.

 How do the rules for scientific communication make it possible for scientists to check each other's work?

SKILLS PRACTICE

Communicating

Use the student notes below to write a lab report. The questions on page 26 will help you with the main sections of the report. You will need a sheet of graph paper.

While Tom carried out a science investigation, he wrote the following information in his laboratory notebook. Write a lab report for his investigation.

Today we put boiling water into four different containers. I thought the containers with a vacuum would be the best containers for keeping the water hot. Then we measured the temperature of the water in each container.

At first we checked the temperatures every 10 minutes. Later we checked every 20 or 30 minutes. Here's the list of the times when we took temperature readings, in minutes: 10, 20, 30, 40, 60, 90, 120, 150.

We used a Celsius thermometer. Here are the temperatures we found:

First container: 100, 99, 95, 91, 88, 83, 74, 67, 65
Second container: 100, 100, 99, 99, 98, 97, 96, 95, 94
Third container: 100, 97, 94, 91, 88, 82, 75, 68, 65
Fourth container: 100, 99, 98, 97, 97, 95, 94, 93, 92

I think we can use these tests to figure out which container is the best container to use for soup and hot drinks. The containers are the same except for these two differences:

1. The first and second containers have a silver layer in them. The third and fourth containers don't have a silver layer.
2. The second and fourth containers have a vacuum between their layers. The first and third don't have a vacuum between the layers. (A vacuum is a space with the air taken out.)

Communicating *(continued)*

1. Read over Tom's notes on page 25. Write a sentence describing the problem or question that he was investigating.

2. Write out the hypothesis Tom was testing in the investigation. (*Hint:* Try to write the hypothesis as a prediction using the words *If . . . then . . . .*)

3. Make a list of the materials Tom used.

4. Write down the steps in the procedure Tom followed.

5. Organize Tom's observations in a data table. Use the following data table as a guide.

COMPARISON OF FOUR CONTAINERS				
	Temperature (°C)			
Time (min)	**Container 1**	**Container 2**	**Container 3**	**Container 4**

6. Analyze the data by making a graph on graph paper. (*Hint:* Graph *Time* on the horizontal axis and *Temperature* on the vertical axis. Find a clear way to label the data for the four containers—for example, use four different colors.)

7. Write a conclusion based on Tom's data.

8. Explain whether or not the conclusion you wrote supports Tom's hypothesis.

9. Write down some additional questions or ideas that Tom might investigate after completing this lab.

10. **Think About It** Suppose your teacher asked you to give a brief oral summary of Tom's lab to another class. Write down what you would say. Would you use any graphs or illustrations? Explain why or why not.

Inquiry Skills Activity Book I

SKILLS INTRODUCTION

Measuring

If you enjoy sports, you know how exciting it is when an athlete swims faster, runs longer, or hits a ball farther than other competitors. You also know that people aren't satisfied with descriptions like "faster" or "longer"—they want exact statistics showing just how fast an athlete ran and how great the margin of victory was. Measurements can help make sports more fun.

Common SI Units		
Property	**Basic Unit**	**Symbol**
Length	meter	m
Liquid volume	liter	L
Mass	gram	g
Temperature	degree Celsius	°C

Measurements are also important in science because they provide important specific information and help observers avoid bias. **Measuring** is comparing an object or process to a standard. Scientists use a common set of standards, called the International System of Units. This system is often abbreviated as SI (for its French name, *Système International d'Unités*). The table above lists the basic units for four common properties.

The basic unit for length is the meter. For a property such as length, researchers often need to measure amounts that are much smaller or much larger than the basic unit. In the SI system, the smaller or larger units are based on multiples of 10. For example, notice that the meter below is divided into 10 main sections, called decimeters. Each decimeter is then divided into ten sections, called centimeters. That means that a decimeter is $\frac{1}{10}$ (or 0.1) of a meter. A centimeter is $\frac{1}{100}$ (or 0.01) of a meter. A millimeter is $\frac{1}{1,000}$ (or 0.001) of a meter.

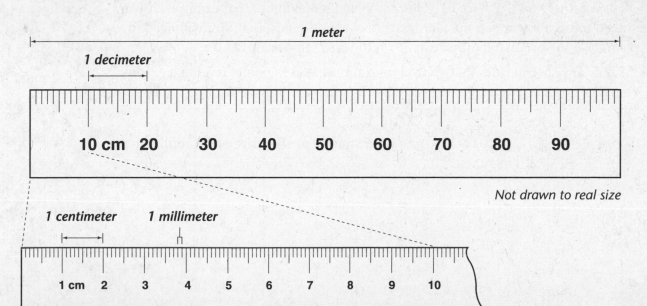

Not drawn to real size

Measuring *(continued)*

The same prefixes that are used for naming smaller and larger units of length are also used for naming different size units of volume and mass. Look at the chart below to see the meaning of some common prefixes.

Common SI Prefixes			
Prefix	**Symbol**	**Meaning**	**Example**
kilo-	k	1,000	kilometer (km)
hecto-	h	100	hectometer (hm)
deka-	da	10	dekameter (dam)
deci-	d	0.1 $(\frac{1}{10})$	decimeter (dm)
centi-	c	0.01 $(\frac{1}{100})$	centimeter (cm)
milli-	m	0.001 $(\frac{1}{1,000})$	millimeter (mm)

 ## Tips for Making Measurements

- ◆ Know the purpose of your measurement. Choose the most suitable size unit, for example, centimeters for a book or meters for the classroom floor.

- ◆ Know how your measuring tool works, for example what main units it measures and what the smaller units mean.

- ◆ Always label your measurements. If you perform any math operations such as adding or subtracting measurements, always label the resulting numbers properly.

- ◆ Determine whether you will need one, two, or a series of measurements. Figure out whether you will have to perform any math operations. For example, if you need to find how much the temperature of a liquid increased, you will need to subtract the original temperature from the final temperature.

- ◆ Know any special rules that apply. For example, read the water level in a graduated cylinder at eye level and at the lowest point of the curved surface.

Reading Checkpoint How could you demonstrate that there are 1,000 millimeters in 1 meter?

SKILLS PRACTICE

Measuring: Length

Write your answers to the questions below in the spaces provided. If you need more space, use a separate sheet of paper.

Length is the distance between two points. Length is usually measured with rulers. Examine the metric ruler diagramed below. Notice that the labeled units are in centimeters (cm). Small vertical lines separate each centimeter into 10 sections. Each of these sections measures 0.1 (or $\frac{1}{10}$) of a centimeter, which equals 1 millimeter (mm). When you use a metric ruler, decide which of these units you will use. For example, if you measure the line in Example 1 in millimeters, you would say it's 19 mm long. If you measure it in centimeters, you would say it's 1.9 cm long.

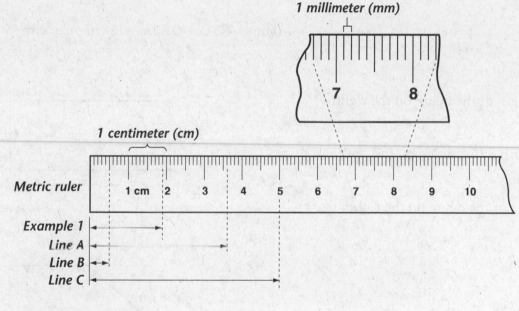

1. How many millimeters long is Line A? _____

2. How many centimeters long is Line A? _____

3. How many millimeters long is Line B? _____

4. How many centimeters long is Line B? _____

5. How many millimeters long is Line C? _____

6. How many centimeters long is Line C? _____

Hint: Did you include the proper unit in each of your measurements? If not, go back and label them.

Name _____ Date _____ Class _____

Measuring: Length *(continued)*

Using Length Measurements to Find Area and Volume

You can use metric measurements to find the area of a figure by multiplying length × width.

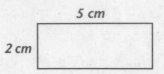

Area = 5 cm × 2 cm = 10 cm^2

You can use metric measurements to find the volume by multiplying length × width × height.

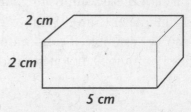

Volume = 5 cm × 2 cm × 2 cm = 20 cm^3

7. What is the length of the figure on the right?

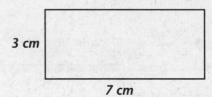

8. What is the width of the figure on the right?

9. What is the area of the figure on the right?

10. What is the volume of the figure on the right?

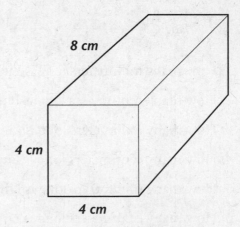

11. Think About It If the measurements of a rectangle are 30 mm by 70 mm, would its area be the same size as the area of the rectangle for Questions 7–9? Explain.

© Pearson Education, Inc., publishing as Pearson Prentice Hall. All rights reserved.

SKILLS PRACTICE

Measuring: Liquid Volume

Write your answers to the questions below in the spaces provided. If you need more space, use a separate sheet of paper.

The volume of an object is the amount of space it takes up. You will often measure the volume of liquids using a graduated cylinder. ("Graduated" means that the cylinder is marked with measurement units.) Always read a graduated cylinder at eye level. Also, water in a graduated cylinder has a curved surface called the meniscus. Read the volume at the bottom of the meniscus.

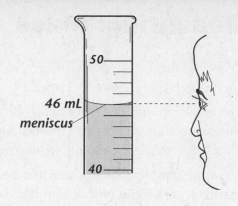

Hints: Always check the unnumbered marks on a graduated cylinder to see how many sections there are and what they measure. Also, sometimes you have to estimate a measurement between two marks. Prove to yourself that both graduated cylinders on the right contain 25 mL.

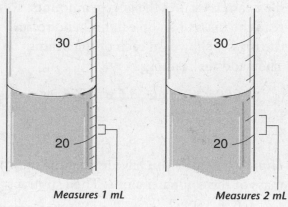

Measures 1 mL   Measures 2 mL

What is the volume of the liquid shown in graduated cylinders 1–4 below? What is the total volume in graduated cylinder 5?

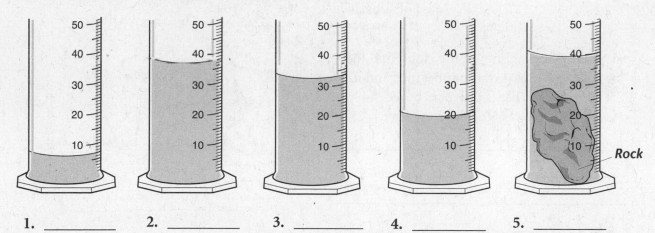

Rock

1. _____   2. _____   3. _____   4. _____   5. _____

6. If the diagrams for Questions 4 and 5 show the same graduated cylinder before and after the rock was added, what can you infer about the volume of the rock?

_____

7. Think About It Describe how you can use a graduated cylinder to measure the volume of an irregular object.

Name _____ Date _____ Class _____

Measuring: Mass

Write your answers to the questions below in the spaces provided. If you need more space, use a separate sheet of paper.

Mass is the amount of matter in an object. There are different kinds of balances used to measure mass. Be sure you understand how your balance works. Some balances give a single reading. Others give two or more readings that you have to add together.

For example, look at the triple-beam balance on the right. Notice that the middle beam measures the largest amounts. To read the mass of an object, find and record the masses shown on each of the beams. Then add the readings.

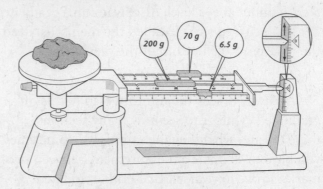

200 g + 70 g + 6.5 g = 276.5 g

Hint: Sometimes you have to find the mass of a substance in a container. Find the mass of the container alone. Then subtract that mass from the combined mass.

Mass of substance and container	29 g
Mass of container	− 13 g
Mass of substance	16 g

1. Using the diagram on the right, find the combined mass of the substance and its container. What is the mass of the substance if the mass of the container is 25 g?

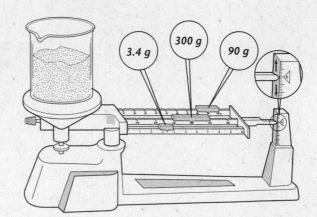

_____

_____

_____

2. What is the mass of a powder if the combined mass of the powder and its container is 12 grams and the mass of the container alone is 4 grams? _____

_____

3. **Think About It** How are the three beams on a triple-beam balance different?

Name _____ Date _____ Class _____

Measuring: Temperature

Write your answers to the questions below in the spaces provided. If you need more space, use a separate sheet of paper.

Temperature is a measure of how hot or cold something is. In science, you will measure temperature with a Celsius thermometer like the one at the right. The correct unit for readings on this thermometer is °C. As you read the temperatures in the first three diagrams below, notice which thermometer marks are labeled and unlabeled, and determine what the unlabeled marks represent. Also, always check whether you are reading temperatures above or below zero. Temperatures below zero should be shown with a minus sign.

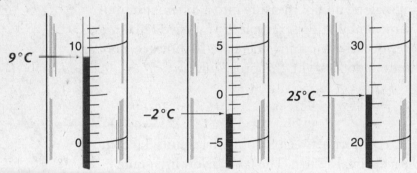

What temperature is shown in each of the diagrams below?

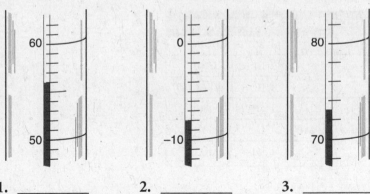

1. _____   2. _____   3. _____

4. Suppose that at 9:00 A.M. the temperature of a room is 18°C, and at noon it is 24°C. What was the increase in temperature?_____

_____

5. If you add ice to water that is at 65°C and the water temperature drops to 40°C, what was the temperature decrease? _____

_____

6. **Think About It** Describe how you found the temperature increase and temperature decrease in Questions 4 and 5.

Calculating

Scientists must often solve problems that involve very large or very small numbers. For example, astronomers study galaxies with millions of stars that are at great distances from Earth. Microbiologists measure organisms or parts of organisms that can be seen only with the most powerful microscopes. Physicists investigate particles that are even smaller. Making calculations is important in the work of these and other scientists. **Calculating** is a process in which a person uses mathematical operations such as addition, subtraction, multiplication, and division to manipulate numbers and symbols.

One important type of calculation you will need to make is converting units of measure. That means changing one unit of measure into a different unit of measure that represents the same amount. For example, if you have 220 dimes, how many dollars do you have? Because you know there are 10 dimes in a dollar, you can easily convert the dimes to dollars with this procedure.

$$220 \text{ dimes} \times \frac{\$1}{10 \text{ dimes}} = \frac{\$220}{10} = \$22$$

In science, you will need to convert between SI, or metric, units. Like the dollar system, the SI system is a decimal system. The table below lists some common metric conversions.

Common Metric Conversions	
Length	1 km = 1,000 m
	1 m = 100 cm
	1 m = 1,000 mm
	1 cm = 10 mm
Liquid volume	1 L = 1,000 mL
Mass	1 kg = 1,000 g

For example, suppose you need to convert 117 millimeters into centimeters. One way to make the conversion is to follow the procedure that was just used to convert dimes to dollars:

$$117 \text{ millimeters} \times \frac{1 \text{ centimeter}}{10 \text{ millimeters}} = \frac{117}{10} \text{ centimeters} = 11.7 \text{ centimeters}$$

Calculating *(continued)*

 Tips for Calculating

Follow these steps when converting between units.

1. Begin by writing down the measurement you want to convert on the left side of the equation. Suppose you want to convert 1.6 liters to milliliters. Write:

1.6 liters ×

2. Write a conversion factor that represents the relationship between the two units you are converting: *1 liter = 1,000 milliliters.* Writing this conversion factor as the correct fraction is an important step.

$$1.6 \text{ liters} \times \frac{1,000 \text{ milliliters}}{1 \text{ liter}}$$

Make sure you place the units you are starting with—liters, in this example—in the denominator. In the next step, you will see why that is important.

3. Multiply the measurement you want to convert by the conversion factor. When you multiply these two terms, the units in the first measurement will cancel out with the units in the denominator. The result will be a fraction.

$$1.6 \cancel{\text{ liters}} \times \frac{1,000 \text{ milliliters}}{1 \cancel{\text{ liter}}} = \frac{1,600.0}{1} \text{ milliliters}$$

4. Divide the numerator of the fraction by the denominator. Your answer will be in the units you are trying to find.

$$1.6 \cancel{\text{ liters}} \times \frac{1,000 \text{ milliliters}}{1 \cancel{\text{ liter}}} = \frac{1,600.0}{1} \text{ milliliters} = 1,600 \text{ milliliters}$$

 Convert between the following units.

3 kilometers = _____ meters

2,082 grams = _____ kilograms

SKILLS PRACTICE

Calculating

Convert between the following units. Fill in your answers in the spaces provided. Show your work below or on a separate sheet of paper.

1. 382 milliliters = _____ liters

2. 2.2 decimeters = _____ millimeters

3. 4.5 meters = _____ centimeters

4. 0.67 liters = _____ milliliters

5. 303 grams = _____ kilograms

6. 3.7 liters = _____ milliliters

7. 4.1 grams = _____ milligrams

8. 211 centimeters = _____ meters

9. 0.5 kilograms = _____ milligrams

10. 17 meters = _____ centimeters

11. **Think About It** Look over all the conversions you just made. Try to find a shortcut method for converting between one metric unit and another, for example, from milliliters to liters. (*Hint:* Examine how the position of the decimal point changed in each example.)

Inquiry Skills Activity Book I

SKILLS INTRODUCTION

Designing an Experiment

Have you ever timed two different routes to school or compared two kinds of shampoo? If you have, you have performed a simple experiment. You probably did not plan your experiment on paper before you carried it out. Scientists, however, design experiments carefully before actually performing them. **Designing an experiment** is making an organized plan to test a hypothesis. An experimental design usually follows a definite pattern. When you design experiments according to this pattern, you will use many individual science skills. Some of these skills are described briefly below.

Pose a Question

Scientists design experiments to answer questions or solve problems. For example, suppose you've heard people say that adding sugar to the water in a vase of flowers keeps the flowers fresh. You wonder whether that statement is true. To find out, you will perform an experiment. You write the topic to be investigated in the form of a scientific question: "Does adding sugar to water keep flowers fresh?"

Develop a Hypothesis

You then write a hypothesis, which is a possible answer to a question or explanation to be tested. A hypothesis can take the form of an *If . . . then . . .* statement. The hypothesis you decide to test in your experiment is *"If I add sugar to the water in a vase, then the flowers will stay fresh longer."*

Plan the Procedure

The procedure describes what you plan to do and identifies the data you plan to collect. Begin by identifying the manipulated variable—the factor you will purposely change—and the responding variable—the factor you predict will change as a result of the manipulated variable. Here, the manipulated variable is the presence or absence of sugar in the water. The responding variable is the length of time that the flowers remain fresh. The procedure is a step-by-step description of how you will change the manipulated variable and observe the effects upon the responding variable. Preparing a data table for recording your observations is a key part of planning the procedure.

Before you begin carrying out the procedure, you must also identify the materials you will need. Write a list of those materials and then continue making your plan. When your plan is complete, revise the materials list, if necessary.

Designing an Experiment *(continued)*

Controlling Variables To be sure that your results are caused only by changes in the manipulated variable, you need to control all other variables that might affect your experiment. Controlling variables means keeping conditions the same. For example, you would keep all the flowers at the same temperature. Other variables you would control include the type and size of the containers, the number of flowers in each container, and the amount of light they receive.

Writing Operational Definitions To enable anyone to repeat and test your experiment, you must write an operational definition for any key term that does not have a single, clear meaning. For example, you could define "remaining fresh" as "flowers keeping their petals." That definition tells anyone how to measure the responding variable.

Interpret the Data

During the experiment, you record all your observations. These observations are your data. Interpreting the data means explaining that data. You may make simple comparisons or look for trends or patterns. For example, if flowers in both groups kept the same number of petals, both groups of flowers stayed fresh the same length of time.

Draw Conclusions

After you interpret the data, you need to compare that interpretation with your hypothesis and decide whether the hypothesis was true or false. This step is called drawing a conclusion. This step may conclude a scientist's investigation, or it may lead the scientist to raise new questions and design new experiments.

 **Reading Checkpoint** Designing an experiment properly can be a challenging task. Why do scientists take the time to plan all the details carefully before beginning work on an experiment?

Name _____ Date _____ Class _____

Posing Questions

Why isn't my radio working? What's the most popular radio program? How does a radio work? What's the best kind of music? These are different kinds of questions you might ask. Some of them concern physical objects. Others are based on values or opinions—what people believe is right or wrong, or beautiful or ugly.

Questions are an essential part of science. But scientific questions are limited to the natural world—to material objects and energy changes you can observe directly or with scientific tools. The objects may be either living or nonliving things. The energy changes may be easy to observe, such as the sound of thunder overhead, or more difficult, such as the light coming from a distant star. What makes a question scientific is that it can be answered by observations, or evidence.

Scientists may start with a broad question such as "Why do people get colds?" Next, they break the question down into smaller questions: Can you catch a cold from someone else? Is there a relationship between getting chills and catching a cold? They state the final question in a way that can be answered by investigation or experiment. A good scientific question is "Does getting chilled cause colds?"

Narrowing down a question often helps researchers plan an investigation and gather evidence to answer the question. For example, to determine whether chills cause colds, a scientist could ask volunteers to undergo low temperatures that produce chills. If few or no volunteers catch colds, the scientist has obtained evidence to answer the question.

 ## Tips for Posing Questions

1. Begin by listing several questions on a topic about the natural world.

2. Try to eliminate questions that cannot be answered by gathering evidence.

3. Break broad questions into questions that can be investigated one at a time.

4. Word questions in a way that allows them to be answered by an investigation or experiment. Here are some good ways to begin scientific questions: "What is the relationship between . . ." "What factors cause . . ." "What is the effect of . . ." Be sure that the question identifies a relationship or factor you can investigate.

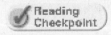 Choose the one question below that can be answered scientifically, and word it in the form of a scientific question.

♦ Which flowers are prettier, daisies or roses?

♦ Can you get warts from handling toads?

♦ Do cats make better pets than dogs?

SKILLS PRACTICE

Posing Questions

Examine the statements below. For each of Questions 1–10, write yes *if the topic can be investigated scientifically. Write* no *if it cannot be investigated scientifically. Then, for each item to which you answered* yes, *rewrite the topic in the form of a scientific question. Answer Question 11 on a separate sheet of paper.*

1. Some people work better in the morning, and other people work better in the afternoon.

    _____

2. Taking something that belongs to another person is wrong.

    _____

3. Snakes travel in pairs.

    _____

4. Animals behave in strange ways before an earthquake.

    _____

5. People who don't recycle should have to pay fines.

    _____

6. Basketball is a better sport than soccer.

    _____

7. You will remember best whatever you read just before you fall asleep.

    _____

8. Maria's kind of bike is faster than Rob's kind of bike.

    _____

9. Each year when the weather gets cold, birds fly to warmer regions.

    _____

10. Trucks use more gasoline than cars.

    _____

11. **Think About It** Choose one of the scientific questions you developed and tell what kind of evidence you would need to answer the question. How do you think a researcher could collect that evidence?

Name _____ Date _____ Class _____

SKILLS INTRODUCTION

Developing a Hypothesis

Suppose you and your neighbor are growing tomatoes. One day you notice that your neighbor's plants are much bigger than yours. What's causing the difference? How can you get your plants to grow as big as your neighbor's?

The question you asked about the tomato plants could lead you to develop a hypothesis. A **hypothesis** (plural: *hypotheses*) is a possible explanation for a set of observations or answer to a scientific question. Hypotheses are based on a person's observations and previous knowledge or experience.

In science, hypotheses must be testable. That means that researchers should be able to carry out an investigation and obtain evidence that shows whether the hypothesis is true or false. The way a hypothesis is written can outline a way to test it. Try to word each of your hypotheses in the form of an *If . . . then . . .* statement.

Read the following three examples. Notice which of these predictions are testable. Also notice how they are worded.

Example 1: If I give my plants fertilizer, then they will grow as big as my neighbor's plants. (testable and properly worded)

Example 2: If I get lucky, then my plants will grow bigger. (not testable, because you can't control "getting lucky")

Example 3: My plants aren't growing bigger because I don't water them enough. (not worded properly)

 ## Tips for Developing Hypotheses

◆ Ideas for hypotheses often result from problems that have been identified or questions that have been raised. To help develop ideas for a hypothesis, write down several questions about the topic. Try to narrow the questions to one that can be investigated scientifically. Then write the hypothesis.

◆ Make sure the hypothesis can be tested through an investigation.

◆ Check the way you worded the hypothesis. Try to word the hypothesis as an *If . . . then . . .* statement.

 Write a hypothesis based on this question: "Will empty trucks use the same amount of gas as heavily loaded trucks?"

SKILLS PRACTICE

Developing a Hypothesis

The day after a picnic, you look into the cooler. All of yesterday's ice has turned to water. Only two beverages are left. A can of diet soda is floating at the surface. A can of regular soda is resting at the bottom.

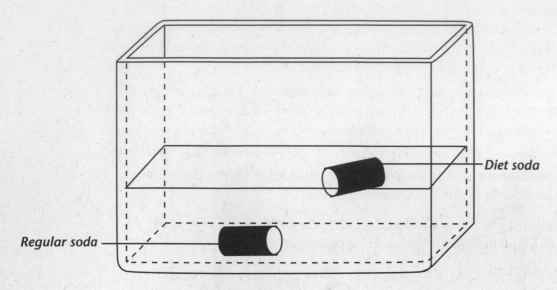

Diet soda

Regular soda

You pick up the two cans. You see that both drinks are made by the same company. Then you read the labels.

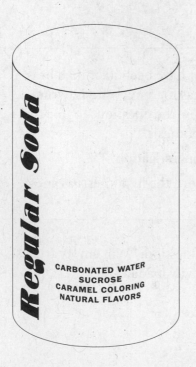

Regular Soda

CARBONATED WATER
SUCROSE
CARAMEL COLORING
NATURAL FLAVORS

Diet Soda

CARBONATED WATER
ASPARTAME
CARAMEL COLORING
NATURAL FLAVORS

Developing a Hypothesis (continued)

Answer the following questions.

1. You think that something about the regular drink must have made it sink, while something about the diet drink made it float. Write down at least two possible factors that could have caused the events.

   _____

   _____

2. Suppose that the type of drink did *not* affect which can floated or sank. Maybe the cans themselves were different in some way. Maybe something besides soda got into one of the cans by mistake. Write down at least two possible factors that could have caused the events.

   _____

   _____

3. Write down any other possible explanations you can think of. Could the cooler have had any affect? Could something in the water be responsible? Could there be an object in the water that you can't see?

   _____

   _____

4. Review your answers to Question 1. Use one of your ideas to write a hypothesis explaining why one can floated and the other sank. (*Hint:* Try to use the words *If. . ., then. . . .*)

   _____

   _____

5. Review your answers to Questions 2 and 3. Choose one of your statements describing something besides the type of drink that caused the floating or sinking. Write a hypothesis based on that idea.

   _____

   _____

6. Are both of your hypotheses testable? Write a brief description of how you could test each one. Mention any equipment you would need. (*Hint:* You can open the cans and pour out the drinks as part of your tests.)

   _____

   _____

7. **Think About It** Review your work. Use it to help you write a short summary of how to develop a hypothesis about an event.

SKILLS INTRODUCTION

Controlling Variables

Suppose that you are planning to try out for the track team. To make the team, you need to increase your speed. You wonder whether to eat a new cereal being advertised for athletes. You could eat the cereal every morning for a month, then run a timed race. If your new time was faster than your previous time, would the cereal be the cause? Based on your test, there'd be no way to know! Too many factors could explain your improved speed. The only way to be sure whether a particular variable causes a specific result is to conduct a controlled experiment.

Every experiment involves several variables, or factors that can change. For example, consider this question: Will houseplants grow faster if you make the room warmer? To answer this question, you decide to grow plants at different temperatures. The variable that you purposely change and test—the temperature of the room—is called the **manipulated variable.** The factor that may change as a result of the manipulated variable—how fast the plants grow—is called the **responding variable.**

An experimental plan is not complete unless the experimenter controls all other variables. **Controlling variables** means keeping all conditions the same except for the manipulated variable. In an experiment on temperature and plant growth, for example, you have to control any other variables that might affect the growth rate. Such variables include the size of the container, the type of soil, the amount of water, the amount of light, and the use of fertilizer. In addition, you would need to use identical plants in the experiment.

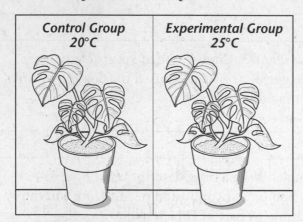

Same kinds of plants
Identical containers
Same type and amount of soil
Same type and amount of fertilizer
Same amount of water
Same lighting

When all these variables are controlled, you can logically conclude that the differences in your results are due to changes in the manipulated variable.

Controlling Variables (continued)

How to Identify the Control Group In a controlled experiment, scientists usually study groups of living or nonliving things instead of comparing just two individual things. The groups that are being studied are called the experimental group and the control group. The experimental group is the group whose conditions are being changed. In the example on the previous page, the plants being grown at the warmer temperature of 25°C make up the experimental group. The control group, or the control, is the group whose conditions are *not* being changed. In the example, the plants grown at the usual temperature of 20°C make up the control group.

The purpose of the control group is to serve as a standard of comparison. For example, if the plants in the control group grew an average of 1 centimeter after 3 weeks, you could compare whether the plants in the experimental group grew the same amount, or grew more than or less than 1 centimeter.

Tips for Controlling Variables

◆ Start by describing the question or process being investigated. Then identify the manipulated variable and the responding variable in the investigation. Predict the kinds of results you might observe in the responding variable.

◆ Create a list of all of the other variables that might affect the responding variable.

◆ Consider whether you have forgotten any of the most common types of variables: time, temperature, length, width, height, mass, volume, number, and the kinds of substances being used in the experiment.

◆ Determine whether or not one of the objects or groups of objects will serve as the control.

 Why must variables in an experiment be controlled?

SKILLS PRACTICE

Controlling Variables

Answer the following questions in the space provided.

1. You are planning an experiment to find out whether the rate at which water freezes depends on the shape of its container. Identify the manipulated variable and the responding variable. List the other variables you would control.

_____

_____

_____

2. Researchers want to determine the best temperature for storing batteries. Describe a possible experiment and list the variables to be controlled in that experiment. Be sure to identify the manipulated and the responding variables.

_____

_____

_____

3. Your friend has to plan an experiment for a science fair. He asks for your help. His topic is "The Strongest Cloth for Backpacks." What variables must his experiment include? What variables must be controlled?

_____

_____

_____

4. Suppose you wanted to compare two different stain removers to learn which one was better at removing food stains from clothing. In your test, what variables would you need to control?

_____

_____

_____

5. **Think About It** Some classmates conducted an experiment to find out which brand of paper towels is the strongest. You find out that they didn't try to control any variables. Write a few sentences explaining why they cannot draw any useful conclusions from their experiment.

_____

_____

_____

Name _____ Date _____ Class _____

Forming Operational Definitions

Suppose that your class and another class work together on an experiment. You're trying to determine what kinds of balls roll the fastest. When the experiment is finished, you all want to compare your data, so you must all perform the experiment in the same way. That means that each time a team of students repeats the experiment, they have to use the same materials and procedure as every other team. They must also make their measurements in an identical manner.

Scientists also repeat investigations—their own and those of other researchers—to be sure that specific data are reliable. To make such repetition possible, scientists use operational definitions. An **operational definition** is a statement that describes how a particular variable is to be measured, or how an object or condition is to be recognized. Operational definitions tell you what to do or what to observe. (The word "operational" means "describing what to do.") Operational definitions need to be clear and precise so that a reader knows exactly what to observe or measure.

In the experiment described above, the two classes could agree on a common procedure: Set up a ramp exactly 10 centimeters high and 2 meters long, and use tape to make a "finish line" at the bottom of the ramp. Make a series of tests by letting two different balls to roll down the ramp at the same time. By using the following definition, the classes would eventually determine which ball rolls the fastest.

Example 1: Operational definition: The fastest ball is the one that crosses the finish line before all the other balls.

When you read or write an operational definition, ask yourself, "Does this definition describe what to do or what to observe?" In the example just given, the student teams would be able to use the procedure and the definition to compare their results. Here are some other examples of operational definitions.

Example 2: Lemon juice, vinegar, and certain other substances are acids. To find out whether a substance is an acid, place a drop of the substance on blue litmus paper. Operational definition: Substances that cause the blue litmus paper to turn pink are acids.

Example 3: To measure a person's pulse, place your index and middle fingers lightly on the inside of the person's wrist and find the beating artery. Operational definition: The pulse is the the number of beats counted in 1 minute.

Example 4: You have to classify vertebrates as fish, amphibians, reptiles, birds, or mammals. Operational definition: A bird is an animal that has two feet, a pair of wings, and feathers.

Example 5: You have to determine the relative ages of layers of sedimentary rock. Operational definition: In sedimentary rock that has not been disturbed, the oldest rock is the bottom layer area, and the youngest rock is the top layer.

It is often possible to write more than one operational definition for a variable. For example, the speed of a moving object can be measured in many ways, such as timed photographs, speedometers, and radar guns. When you write an operational definition, choose a procedure that makes sense for the investigation you're carrying out. Ask yourself: "Will the measurements I obtain with this definition give me data that help me test my hypothesis or answer my question?" If the answer is no, you need to rethink and revise your definition.

 ## Tips for Writing Operational Definitions

♦ Look over the written plan for carrying out an investigation, or write up a plan.

♦ Identify and list any variables or terms that do not have a single, clear, obvious meaning.

♦ If there are several reasonable ways to make an observation or to perform an action, choose one that suits the purpose of the investigation.

♦ Write a clear, complete definition of what the researcher should do or measure. Check your definition by asking yourself, "Will this definition tell another person what to observe or how to measure?" If necessary, revise your definition before starting your investigation.

 Why are operational definitions important in science?

SKILLS PRACTICE

Forming Operational Definitions

Write an operational definition for each underlined idea in the space provided.

1. <u>On a cold day,</u> let the water in the pan freeze outdoors.

   _____

   _____

   _____

2. You will test these two fertilizers to determine which one helps <u>plants grow faster.</u>

   _____

   _____

   _____

3. Rearrange the list of zoo animals in order of their size, <u>with the biggest ones first.</u>

   _____

   _____

   _____

4. People who take a driver's education course are probably <u>better drivers</u> than drivers who do not.

   _____

   _____

   _____

5. When you finish working on an experiment, <u>wash your hands thoroughly.</u>

   _____

   _____

   _____

6. **Think About It** A good operational definition tells a person clearly how to perform an observation or take a measurement. Choose one of your definitions and explain whether you think other people would be able to follow the directions you provided.

   _____

   _____

INTRODUCING THE SKILL

Interpreting Data

Suppose your class is planning a party. You don't have lots of money to spend, so you're looking for bargains as you buy the food, drinks, and decorations. For example, you can buy soft drinks in separate cans, in packs of six cans, or in one-liter bottles. Some stores are having sales, and you also have a few money-saving coupons. To figure out the best price, you would first have to decide how many soft drinks you need, list all the price information you have, and then compare the various choices. That's similar to what you do when you analyze data in a science investigation.

During a science investigation, you make observations and take measurements that are called **data.** For example, you might observe color changes in a liquid or measure the temperature of objects left out in a sunny spot. After you collect your data, you need to interpret—or find meaning in—the data by looking for patterns or trends.

Suppose that scientists recorded the temperature at a specific location on Earth's surface. After that, they drilled below the surface to collect temperatures at different depths. The results of their work are shown in the table below.

Depth (km)	Temperature (°C)
0	15
1	52
2	88
3	120
4	151
5	179
6	206
7	232
8	257

By looking at the table, you can see that the deeper the location of the measurement, the higher the temperature. But it's hard to find any more details about that trend by just examining the table. So you decide to graph the data.

Interpreting Data *(continued)*

You could use the data to create a graph like this one. You could then interpret the graph and make inferences like the ones that follow.

Example 1: The deeper the location of the temperature reading beneath Earth's surface, the hotter the temperature is.

Example 2: For every additional kilometer of depth, the temperature increases about 30 Celsius degrees.

Example 3: The temperature at a depth of 3.5 km would be about 135°C.

To determine whether your interpretation of the data is logical, you compare it with what you already know. You know that lava from inside Earth sometimes erupts from volcanoes, and that lava is extremely hot. You decide your interpretation of the data makes sense.

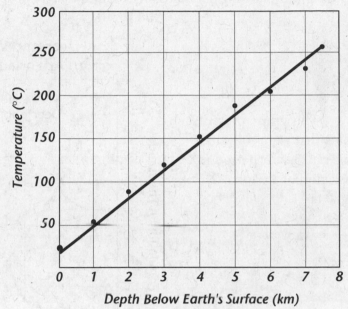

Depth Below Earth's Surface (km)

▶ Tips for Interpreting Data

◆ Organize the data into a table or arrange the data in a specific order, such as largest to smallest. If applicable, make calculations such as adding, subtracting, or finding averages.

◆ Make a graph of the data.

◆ Look for trends or patterns in the data or graph.

◆ Make one or more inferences from the data. Then compare the inferences with what you already know about the topic.

◆ If your inferences seem to contradict what you know, review your work to see whether you made any errors or need to examine the data again.

 Could you use the data about temperatures beneath Earth's surface to predict the temperature at 9 km beneath Earth's surface? Explain your reasoning.

SKILLS PRACTICE

Interpreting Data

Answer the following questions on a separate sheet of paper.

This graph presents data that were collected over a 25-year period in a region of Arizona.

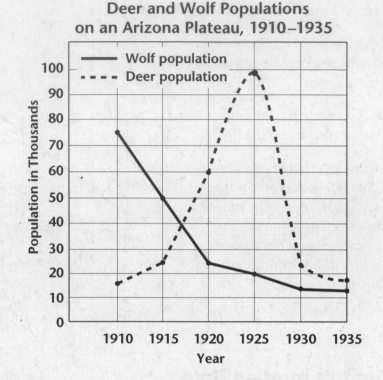

Deer and Wolf Populations on an Arizona Plateau, 1910–1935

1. Start by summarizing the data. Using the title and the axis labels as a guide, write a sentence describing what the data show.

2. Examine the wolf graph. How big was the wolf population in 1910? (*Hint:* Remember to multiply the numbers on the vertical axis by 1,000.)

3. What does the shape of the wolf graph tell you about the wolf population from 1910 to 1935?

4. Examine the deer graph. How big was the deer population in 1910?

5. What does the shape of the deer graph tell you about the deer population from 1910 to 1935?

6. List two other facts that you can learn from the graph.

7. How can the changes shown in this graph be explained?

8. Does your explanation in Question 7 fit in with what you know about deer and wolves? Explain.

9. **Think About It** Look back over your work. Make a list of the steps you took as you interpreted the data in the graph.

SKILLS INTRODUCTION

Drawing Conclusions

Suppose that you have a portable radio with headphones. One day you turn the radio on, but you don't hear your favorite station. You try other stations and still get no sound. You think that the batteries must be dead, so you put in new ones. Still there is no sound. You try replacing your headphones with ones from your sister's radio. Your favorite music is back! You draw the conclusion that there was something wrong with your headphones.

In everyday language, the word "conclusion" means an explanation or interpretation of an observation or a statement. In science, the word "conclusion" usually has a more limited meaning. **Drawing a conclusion** means making a statement summing up what you have learned from an experiment.

The conclusion of an experiment is usually related to the hypothesis. You may recall that a hypothesis is a possible explanation that is tested during an experiment. After you have carried out the procedure, made and recorded observations, and interpreted the data, you can finally determine whether your experiment showed your hypothesis to be true or false.

Suppose that Leon and Jobelle each write a hypothesis about the summer temperatures where they live.

Example 1: Leon writes, *If I measure the temperature on sunny summer days in this location, then the warmest air temperatures will occur between 11 A.M. and 1 P.M.*

Example 2: Jobelle writes, *If the day is sunny, then the hottest time of the day will be about 3 o'clock in the afternoon.*

They then test their hypotheses by measuring the outdoor temperature several times a day for the month of July. Then they average their data and graph the data as shown at the right.

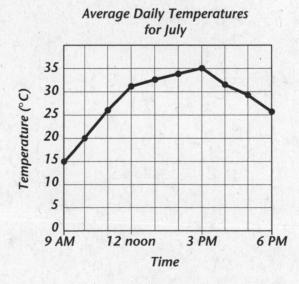

Average Daily Temperatures for July

Drawing Conclusions *(continued)*

From the graph, Leon can see that the results of the investigation do not support his hypothesis. He draws this conclusion: *Based on a study of temperatures between 9 A.M. and 6 P.M. on sunny days, the warmest temperatures do not occur between 11 A.M. and 1 P.M. but happen sometime later in the afternoon.*

The results do support Jobelle's hypothesis, however. She draws the following conclusion: *On sunny days in July, the warmest temperatures occur about 3 P.M.*

Before scientists become confident of their conclusions, they often repeat their experiments many times and compare their work with that of others. Additional experiments may provide further support for a particular hypothesis. Alternatively, they may cause a researcher to revise or replace the hypothesis.

 ## Tips for Drawing Conclusions

- Refer to the hypothesis for your experiment.

- Review the observations in your experiment. Analyze the data, completing whatever calculations or graphs will help you identify trends or patterns in your results.

- Determine whether your data support your hypothesis or suggest that it is false. Write a statement summing up what your results show.

- Consider whether you might plan other experiments to support your conclusion or compare your work with that done by other researchers.

 Do you think Jobelle can use the data to draw a conclusion about daily temperature changes that occur at other times of the year? Explain.

Inquiry Skills Activity Book I

SKILLS PRACTICE

Drawing Conclusions

Answer the questions below on a separate sheet of paper.

Olena and Bruce are studying whether the color of a container affects how fast the container cools down. Olena wrote this hypothesis: *If you put hot water in white and black cans, the cans will cool down at the same rate.* Bruce wrote this hypothesis: *If hot water is put in black and white cans, the black can will cool down faster than the white can.* They then tested their hypotheses. Here is their graph.

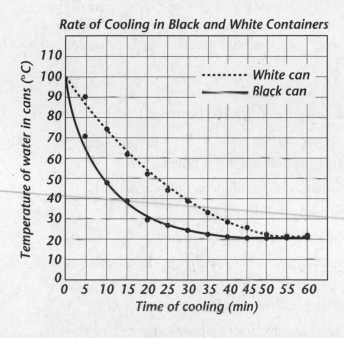

1. Examine the data presented in the graph. Notice the temperatures of the black and white cans at the times the measurements were taken. What does this data tell you about the way the two cans cooled down?

2. Compare the evidence in the graph with Olena's hypothesis. What conclusion should Olena draw?

3. Compare the evidence in the graph with Bruce's hypothesis. What conclusion should Bruce draw?

4. Neither Bruce or Olena included anything about the cans' final temperatures in their hypotheses. Rewrite one of their conclusions to include information about the final temperatures of the cans.

5. **Think About It** Who do you think learned more about temperature changes: Bruce or Olena? Does it make any difference if one person's hypothesis was shown to be false? Explain.

Name _____ Date _____ Class _____

Designing an Experiment

Choose a question from the list below as a topic for an experiment. Alternatively, pose a scientific question of your own and obtain your teacher's approval to use that question.

Remember, as one of the first steps in planning your investigation, you may need to narrow your original question. Then write a hypothesis and design an experiment to answer the question. Be sure to include all the necessary parts of an experiment, such as naming the manipulated and responding variables and identifying the variables you will control. Write any operational definitions that are needed. Include a data table you could use for recording your observations. Use a separate sheet of paper for your work.

1. How is heart rate affected by exercise?

2. How are bean seedlings affected by water that has been polluted by detergent?

3. What effect does acid rain have on marble statues?

4. Does sand in the wheels of my in-line skates affect how fast they roll?

5. Will a wet sheet become dry when hung outdoors on a freezing day?

6. Is a family's health affected by using a dishwasher?

7. How is gas mileage affected by the type of gasoline used?

8. Does the presence of plants growing on a hillside change the amount of soil erosion?

9. Does cold water freeze faster than hot water?

10. Does the type of shampoo I use have an effect on how long my hair stays clean?

11. **Think About It** Review the experiment you just designed. What are some practical problems you might encounter if you carried out the experiment? What could you do to solve one of those problems?

SKILLS INTRODUCTION

Creating Data Tables

Suppose that your class decides to sponsor a Scrabble® competition to raise money. You'll ask people to pay $1.00 each to play. The money will go to a charity that your class has chosen. To keep track of the results, all players will have official score cards that show the number of games they play, their wins and losses, their game scores, and their average score. The easiest way to show all that information would be in a data table.

A **data table** is an organized arrangement of information in labeled rows and columns. Data tables are helpful in many kinds of situations. In science, they are particularly useful when you record observations during an investigation. Making data tables may also help you interpret information that someone else has collected.

Planning a data table is an important part of designing an experiment. A data table provides an orderly way for you to record observations. It can help you keep complete records by reminding you of everything you need to observe. Also, data tables can provide spaces for the results of calculations you plan to do as you interpret the data.

When you create a data table, start by identifying the manipulated and responding variables. For example, suppose you are comparing two types of fertilizer to see whether one of them makes plants grow taller. Your manipulated variable is the type of fertilizer. Your responding variable is the height of the plants. You decide you will measure the height of the plants once a day for a period of three weeks. You also decide to include a control, a plant that receives no fertilizer. You might make a table like the one below.

Effects of Fertilizer on Plant Growth			
Time (days)	**Height of Plant (cm)**		
	Control Plant (no fertilizer)	**Fertilizer A**	**Fertilizer B**
Day 1			
Day 2			
Day 3			

Creating Data Tables *(continued)*

Check your plan to be sure that your data table has a column for each kind of information you will observe and a row for each occasion when you'll make an observation. Be sure to label the columns and rows accurately and identify the units of measurement you are using. And be sure to give the data table a title.

Review the draft of your table to be sure it has places for all the data you plan to collect. For example, in an experiment on the effects of plant fertilizer, you might want to insert columns to record the daily temperature or additional changes in the plants, such as the number of leaves that develop. When your review is complete, create the final data table in your notebook.

 ## Tips for Creating Data Tables

◆ Consider the manipulated and responding variables to determine what observations you will be making.

◆ If you plan to make observations according to a regular pattern, such as once a day, once an hour, or once every five minutes, plan to show those times in the data table.

◆ Make a draft of your table. Show all the columns and rows you'll need and what labels they will have. Be sure to write a title for your table.

◆ Insert units into the column labels where they are needed.

◆ Compare the draft of the data table to the plan for your experiment to be sure you have a place to record all observations you expect to make.

◆ Revise the draft of your data table and draw the final table in your notebook.

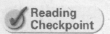 How can a well-organized data table help you keep complete records during an experiment?

SKILLS PRACTICE

Creating Data Tables

Read over the notebook page shown below. Then answer the questions that follow in the spaces provided or on a separate sheet of paper.

Maria did not make a data table before she began her science investigation, but she wrote these notes.

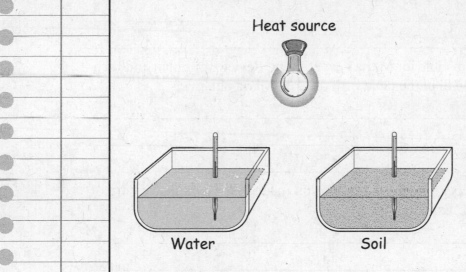

To find out whether water or land gets hotter or cooler in the sun, I will set up a pan of water and a pan of soil. I will put a light bulb halfway between the two pans, and each pan will have a thermometer in it. I will leave the light on for ten minutes and measure the temperature in each pan once every minute.

Heat source

Water   Soil

Here are the results I got. The soil temperatures measured in °C were 20.0, 21.0, 22.0, 23.0, 24.0, 26.0, 27.0, 28.5, 30.0, 31.0, 32.0. Then I turned the light off, and the temperatures were 32.0, 31.0, 30.5, 29.5, 28.0, 27.0, 26.0, 25.0, 23.5, 22.0.

The water temperatures were 20.0, 20.5, 21.0, 21.5, 22.0, 22.0, 22.5, 22.5, 23.0, 23.0. After I turned off the light, the temperatures were 23.0, 22.5, 22.5, 22.0, 22.0, 22.0, 21.5, 21.0, 21.0, 20.5.

Creating Data Tables (continued)

1. Think about Maria's plan. What does the light bulb represent? What do the pans of soil and water represent?

   _____

   _____

   _____

2. What is the manipulated variable in Maria's experiment? What is the responding variable?

   _____

   _____

   _____

3. Would Maria need to consider any other variable(s) as she created a data table for this lab? Explain.

   _____

   _____

   _____

4. Draft a plan for a data table for Maria's experiment. Review your plan and then create the data table. Fill in the table with the data Maria obtained.

   _____

   _____

   _____

5. **Think About It** Examine the data table you made. Is it a complete record of Maria's investigation? Explain.

   _____

   _____

   _____

   _____

Inquiry Skills Activity Book I

SKILLS INTRODUCTION

Creating Bar Graphs

Each day, some students are absent from school because of illness or other factors. Suppose you are given a list of the number of students absent in Grades 6 through 9 today. You are asked to graph the data so that the principal can easily compare the absences across the grades. Which type of graph should you use: bar, circle, or line?

Today's Absences	
Grade	**Number**
6	7
7	9
8	12
9	4

The type of graph you should make depends on your data. Here, the absences in each grade are distinct, or separate, categories. For example, the number of 9th grade absences is distinct from the number of 8th grade absences. You should make a bar graph.

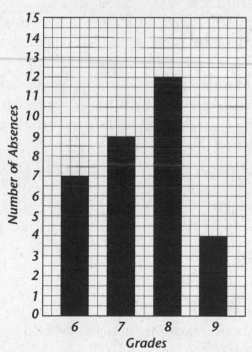

Today's Absences

A bar graph is a diagram in which data about separate but related items are represented by rectangular shapes called bars. You usually place the categories being studied on the horizontal axis. Place the measurements or amounts on the vertical axis. The measurement for each category is represented by a separate bar. The length of the bar indicates the amount of the measurement.

Constructing Bar Graphs *(continued)*

In science, bar graphs usually have simple rectangular shapes to indicate the measurements. Sometimes in newspaper and magazines, bar graphs use drawings that represent the measurements. For example, each absent student could be represented by the drawing of a person. For larger numbers, a drawing could stand for 10 students. But regardless of the way the measurement is represented, bar graphs make it easy to read and compare the separate but related data.

 ## Tips for Constructing Bar Graphs

1. Organize your data in a table. A table makes it easier for you to construct a graph.

2. Draw horizontal and vertical axes on a sheet of graph paper.

3. Place the category being studied, or the manipulated variable, on the horizontal axis. Place the measurements that have been made, or the responding variable, on the vertical axis. Label both axes.

4. Determine the scale for the measurements to be shown on the vertical axis. Choose a scale that lets you represent all the values in your data table. Each square on the graph paper will represent a certain amount. All squares have the same value. In the example on the previous page, each square represents one absent student.

5. On the horizontal axis, show a bar for each category being represented. Use an equal number of squares for the width of each bar and leave a space of at least one square between the bars. In this example, three squares are used for each bar. A space of two squares has been left between the bars.

6. Using your data, draw in the bars. Remember, all the bars must have the same width.

7. Write a title for your bar graph.

 Which of the following examples would you show in a bar graph?

(1) the average weight of a dog during each year of its life

(2) the numbers of dogs, cats, birds, fish, and other pets people cared for during the previous year

Explain your answer.

SKILLS PRACTICE

Creating Bar Graphs

Answer the questions below on a separate sheet of paper. Use a sheet of graph paper to make the graph.

The table below shows the relative diameters of the planets in our solar system in Earth units. That means that Earth is represented as having a diameter of 1 Earth unit. The planet Uranus, which has a diameter that is four times the size of Earth's diameter, is represented by 4 Earth units. The planets are listed in order of their distance from the sun. Mercury is the closest, and Pluto is the farthest away.

Diameters of the Planets in Earth Units	
Planet	**Diameter in Earth Units**
Mercury	0.40
Venus	0.95
Earth	1.00
Mars	0.50
Jupiter	11.20
Saturn	9.50
Uranus	4.00
Neptune	3.90
Pluto	0.20

1. On which axis will you place the names of the planets? (*Hint:* The planets are similar to a category being studied, or a manipulated variable. List the planets in the same order as in the table, starting with Mercury.)

2. Notice that the measurements you need to represent include some numbers between 0 and 1, with the largest number between 11 and 12. What scale will you use to represent the planet diameters? (*Hint:* You may need to estimate the height of certain bars.)

3. On a sheet of graph paper, make a bar graph that displays the data in the table.

4. **Think About It** Suppose you made a bar graph showing the planets' distances from the sun, and you listed them in the same order as in this graph. How would the new graph be similar to the graph you just made? How would it be different?

SKILLS INTRODUCTION

Creating Line Graphs

A science class studying frogs counted the number of times the frogs croaked at different temperatures. The results are shown in the data table on the right. To help interpret that data, the class then created a line graph. A **line graph** is used to display data that show how one variable (the responding variable) changes in response to another variable (the manipulated variable). You should use a line graph when your manipulated variable is continuous, that is, when there are other measurements possible between the ones you tested. For example, in this experiment, temperature is a continuous variable since 27°C is between 26° and 28°, and 22.5°C is between 22° and 23°. Temperature, time, mass, and velocity are just a few examples of continuous variables.

Number of Croaks vs. Temperature	
Air Temperature in °C	**Frog Croaks per Minute**
22	12
23	14
24	15
26	16
28	17
31	21
32	26

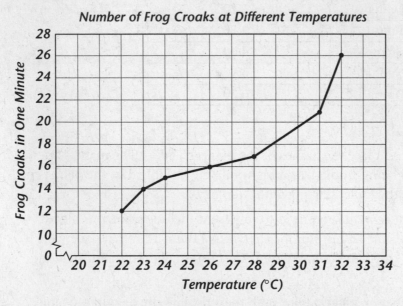

A line graph is a powerful tool because it shows a relationship between two variables. Here, the line graph shows how the number of frog croaks per minute changes as temperature changes. Line graphs also allow you to identify trends and relationships in the data, and thus infer values you did not actually measure. For example, you can infer that at 30°C, the frogs might make 20 croaks per minute. At 20°C, they might make about 10 croaks per minute. (To find out whether these inferences were true, you would have to do additional research.)

Creating Line Graphs *(continued)*

What Is a Best Fit Line Graph? Notice that unlike the graph on page 64, the lines on the graphs below were not drawn from point to point. Instead, the graphs are smooth and continuous. They flow through as many of the data points as possible but do not necessarily touch all the points. This kind of graph is called a "best fit graph." A best fit graph shows an average, a trend, or a pattern in the data.

You may wonder how scientists know when to use a best fit graph. As you continue to study science, you will see that certain kinds of graphs commonly result from scientific experiments. The graphs shown below are three examples.

The first graph shows a straight line, or linear relationship. (Notice that the word *linear* comes from the word *line.*) You can read that straight-line graph to see that as the volume of a liquid (the manipulated variable) increases, the mass of that liquid (the responding variable) also increases.

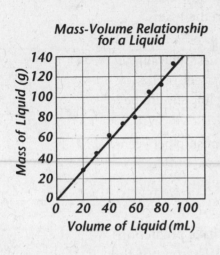

Mass-Volume Relationship for a Liquid

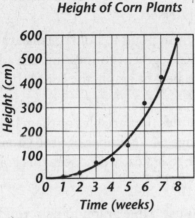

Height of Corn Plants

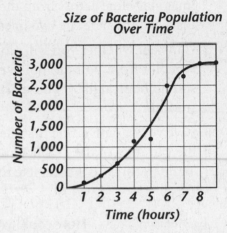

Size of Bacteria Population Over Time

The graphs in the center and on the right are described as nonlinear, meaning they are not straight lines. The center graph shows a curve that continues to rise. You can read that graph to see that over time (the manipulated variable), a corn plant's height (the responding variable) continues to increase.

The graph on the right shows a curve that rises and then flattens out. Here, as time (the manipulated variable) passes, the size of the bacteria population (the responding variable) increases steadily until it reaches a certain size. Then, the size of the population becomes constant.

Look for these and other patterns as you examine additional graphs. Recognizing the pattern of a graph will help you to understand the actual events it represents.

Creating Line Graphs *(continued)*

 ## Tips for Creating Line Graphs

1. On graph paper, draw a horizontal, or *x*-, axis and a vertical, or *y*-, axis.

2. Label the horizontal axis with the name of the manipulated variable. Label the vertical axis with the name of the responding variable. Include the units of measure.

3. Create a scale on each axis by marking off equally-spaced numbers along the axis. Begin with zero or a number slightly less than the smallest number to be graphed. Be sure that each scale covers the entire range of data collected for that variable. Label the units on each scale.

4. Plot each point where the variables intersect. You can do this by following an imaginary line up from the measurement on the *x*-axis. Then follow a second imaginary line across from the corresponding measurement on the *y*-axis. Place a dot where the two lines intersect.

5 Consider whether you will plot from point to point or make a best fit graph. If you plot from point to point, each segment connecting two adjacent points should be straight. If you make a best fit graph, the connecting line should be smooth.

6. Give your graph a title that identifies the variables or the relationship between the variables in the graph. On page 64, "Number of Frog Croaks at Different Temperatures" is a complete title that clearly describes this graph.

 How could you use a line graph to help you make predictions about data that were not actually measured? Use one of the graphs on page 64 or 65 to help you answer this question.

SKILLS PRACTICE

Creating Line Graphs

Use a sheet of graph paper to make a graph of the data given below. Then answer the questions that follow on a separate sheet of paper.

Time vs. Temperature for Unknown Substance		
Time (min)	**Temperature (°C)**	**Solid, Liquid or Gas**
0	−20	Solid
5	0	Solid (melting)
10	0	Solid (melting)
15	52	Liquid
20	100	Liquid (boiling)
25	100	Liquid (boiling)
30	100	Liquid (boiling)
35	100	Liquid (boiling)
40	100	Liquid (boiling)
45	100	Liquid (boiling)
50	100	Liquid (boiling)
55	100	Liquid (boiling)
60	100	Liquid (boiling)
65	100	Liquid (boiling)
70	100	Liquid (boiling)
75	110	Gas
80	120	Gas

A group of researchers were investigating the properties of an unknown substance. They decided to heat the material to study its melting and boiling behavior. They heated a 1-kg sample of the solid material at a steady rate. They measured and recorded the temperature of the sample every 5 minutes.

1. On a sheet of graph paper, make a line graph of the data the group collected.

2. What does the graph tell you about the temperature of the substance at different times during the investigation?

3. **Think About It** Use the information from the third column of the data table to explain what is happening during the various sections of your graph.

Name _____ Date _____ Class _____

Creating Circle Graphs

Suppose that you order an eight-slice pizza for yourself and two friends. The illustration below shows how many pieces each person eats.

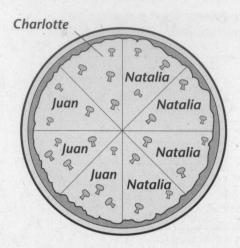

You can change this illustration into a circle graph. A **circle graph** shows data as parts of a whole. The circle represents the whole, or total. The wedges, or segments, represent the parts. Because it resembles a pie cut into slices, a circle graph is sometimes called a pie graph or pie chart.

If you change the pizza illustration into a circle graph, the whole circle will represent the complete pizza. The segments of the graph will show the part of the pizza that each person ate. Look at the data table to see how the number of pieces can be changed into percentages. In a circle graph, all of the parts add up to the total, or 100%.

Amount of Pizza Eaten		
Person	**Number of Pieces**	**Percent of Pizza**
Natalia	4	50%
Juan	3	37.5%
Charlotte	1	12.5%

Like bar graphs, circle graphs can be used to display data in a number of separate categories. Unlike bar graphs, however, circle graphs can be used only when you have data for all the categories that make up the whole.

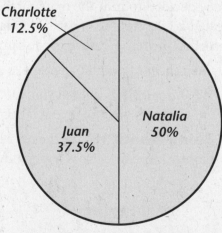

Portion of Pizza Eaten

Creating Circle Graphs (continued)

▶ Tips for Making Circle Graphs

1. Organize your data into a table or list. For example, the data table on the right shows information about 200 ads shown on children's TV shows.

Kinds of Ads on Children's TV Shows	
Type of Product	Number of Ads
Toys	70
Breakfast foods	50
Fast food and drinks	50
Other products	30

2. To find the size of the wedge for each type of product, set up a proportion. Let x equal the number of degrees in that wedge. Then cross-multiply and solve for x. Since there are 360 degrees in a circle, each proportion will read as shown on the right:

$$\frac{\text{Number of ads for product type}}{\text{Total number of ads}} = \frac{x}{360°}$$

For toys: $\dfrac{70}{200} = \dfrac{x}{360°}$

$$70 \times 360° = x \times 200$$

$$\frac{70 \times 360°}{200} = x$$

$$126° = x$$

Number of Ads	70	50	50	30
Size of Wedge	126°	90°	90°	54°

3. Use a compass to draw a circle. Mark the center of the circle. Then use a straightedge to draw a line from the center point to the top of the circle.

4. Use a protractor to measure the angle of the first wedge, using the line you just drew as the 0° line. For example, the wedge for Toys is 126°. Draw a line from the center of the circle to the edge for the angle you measured.

5. Write a label on the wedge to show what it represents. If there is not enough space in the wedge, write the label outside the circle and draw a line to the wedge.

6. Continue around the circle, drawing in and labeling the other wedges. For each new wedge, use the edge of the last wedge as your 0° line.

7. Determine the percentage that each wedge represents by dividing the number of degrees in the wedge by 360°.

For toys: $\dfrac{126°}{360°} \times 100\% = 35\%$

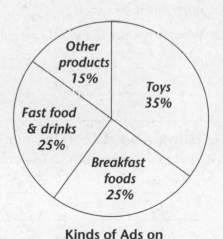

Kinds of Ads on Children's TV Shows

If you add up the number of degrees in all the wedges of a circle graph, what is the total? If you add up all the percentages, what is the total?

SKILLS PRACTICE

Creating Circle Graphs

To complete this activity, you will need a compass and a protractor. Use those tools to answer Question 1 on a separate sheet of paper. Answer the remaining questions in the spaces below.

A middle school class surveyed 500 families who own pets. The data table below shows what kinds of pets the families own. Create a circle graph to display the data.

Kinds of Pets Owned by Families	
Pet	**Number of Families**
Dogs	180
Cats	160
Birds	25
Fish	25
*Other	110

* Includes gerbils, hamsters, rabbits,
guinea pigs, and ferrets

1. Make a circle graph to display the data in this table. (*Hint:* You can round off numbers if you wish.)

2. What are some facts you can learn by examining the graph?

_____

_____

_____

3. **Think About It** Think about the process of creating a circle graph. Why might circle graphs be a less exact way of displaying data than bar graphs?

_____

_____

_____

_____

_____

SKILLS ASSESSMENT

Skills Test A: Basic Process Skills

Questions 1–4: Read each statement. If the statement is an observation, write "O" on the line at the left. If the statement is an inference, write "I" on the line at the left.

_____ **1.** I hear a dog barking.

_____ **2.** In two weeks, there will be snow on the ground.

_____ **3.** The temperature today is 4°C.

_____ **4.** I smell smoke coming from the pile of wood.

Questions 5–8: Write the letter of the correct answer on the line at the left.

_____ **5.** Which of the following is an observation that can be made from the illustration at the right?
  a. Bird A had to fly a great distance to find food.
  b. Bird A is carrying a worm in its mouth.

_____ **6.** Which of the following is an inference that can reasonably be made from evidence in the illustration?
  a. The hole in the tree contains a nest.
  b. Birds A and B do not have enough food to eat.

_____ **7.** Which of the following is a quantitative observation?
  a. Bird A's beak is 35 mm long.
  b. Bird B eats worms.

_____ **8.** Which of the following statements about observations is true?
  a. Only scientists can make accurate observations.
  b. Observations always involve gathering evidence through the senses.

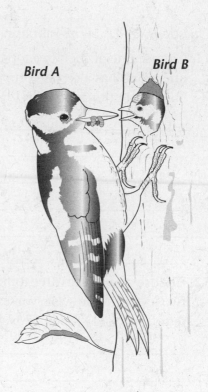

Bird A   *Bird B*

Skills Test A: Basic Process Skills (continued)

Questions 9–10: Write the letter of the correct answer on the line at the left.

_____ 9. Which of the following examples shows a classification system in which one group has a certain property, but the other group does not have that property?
   a. rainy weather; hot weather
   b. materials that dissolve in water; materials that do not dissolve in water

_____ 10. Which of the following classification systems is based on a single idea?
   a. living things; animals that live in water
   b. substances that burn; substances that do not burn

Questions 11–12: Write your answers in the spaces below or on the back of this sheet.

11. Choose one of the three topics given. Create a classification system in which one group has a certain property. The other group does not have that property. Topics: (1) things that fly, (2) musical instruments, (3) sports equipment

_____

_____

_____

_____

_____

12. Choose one of the three topics given, and create a classification system with two levels. If you wish, you can use a diagram to show your classification system. Topics: (1) foods, (2) vehicles people use for travel, (3) pets

_____

_____

_____

_____

Name _____ Date _____ Class _____

Skills Test A: Basic Process Skills *(continued)*

Questions 13–14: Examine the diagrams. Then answer each question by writing the correct answer on the line at the left.

Marcia Stuart is responsible for planning the seating arrangements for a teachers' lunch. As part of her planning, she has made these two diagrams.

For Each Individual's Place

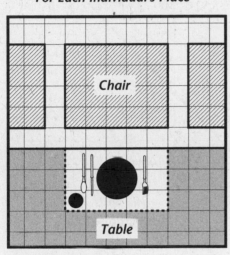

One Whole Table

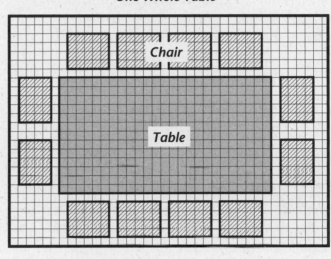

▢ = 10 cm by 10 cm   ▢ = 10 cm by 10 cm

_____ **13.** Marcia's diagrams are examples of ____?____-dimensional models.

_____ **14.** The labels for measurements on the diagrams show that Marcia was trying to make the models in proportion to the actual objects, or to ____?____.

Questions 15–16: Use the diagrams to answer each question in the space provided.

15. Marcia's friend Julio looked at the models and said, "Your plan won't work. You can't put two people at each end of the table." Is Julio right? Explain.

_____

_____

_____

16. Why do you think Marcia made models like these as she planned the seating for the lunch?

_____

_____

Skills Test A: Basic Process Skills *(continued)*

Questions 17–18: Read the paragraph below and examine the graph. Then answer each question on the line at the left.

   A scientist heated an expandable rubber container. As the container was heated, the gas inside expanded. The scientist measured the container's size at every temperature increase of 10 degrees and then graphed the data as shown at the right.

_____ **17.** Determine the size of the container when the temperature is 25°C.

_____ **18.** Predict what the container size would be if the temperature were 60°C.

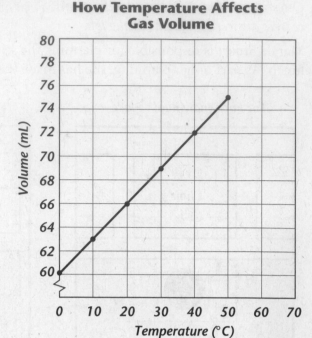

How Temperature Affects Gas Volume

Questions 19–25: Use the following student notes to match the correct information from Column 2 with each item in Column 1. Write the letter of the correct answer on the line at the left.

   I investigated yeast, tiny organisms that give off carbon dioxide gas as they grow. In two bottles, I put 2 mL of yeast, 5 mL of sugar, and water. In Bottle A, I used 250 mL of cold water (20°C). In Bottle B, I used 250 mL of warm water (40°C). I attached a balloon to each bottle. After five minutes, I observed bubbles forming on the surface inside both bottles, and the balloons on both bottles expanded. The balloon on Bottle B became about twice as large as the balloon on Bottle A.

Column 1 Sections of a Lab Report

_____ **19.** Problem or Question

_____ **20.** Hypothesis

_____ **21.** Materials

_____ **22.** Procedure

_____ **23.** Observations

_____ **24.** Analysis

_____ **25.** Conclusion

Column 2 Information to Use in a Lab Report

a. If you increase the water temperature, then the yeast will give off more gas.

b. After five minutes, Balloons A and B expanded. Balloon B expanded more than Balloon A.

c. Yeast give off more gas at higher temperatures.

d. What factors help yeast to grow?

e. Balloon B became bigger than Balloon A, so that means that the yeast in Balloon B gave off more gas.

f. Combine the yeast, sugar and water in a bottle. Put a balloon on the bottle.

g. Yeast, sugar, warm and cool water, containers, timer

Name _____ Date _____ Class _____

SKILLS ASSESSMENT

Skills Test B: Measuring and Calculating

Questions 1–5. Use the diagram below to answer each question. Write your answer on the line at the left.

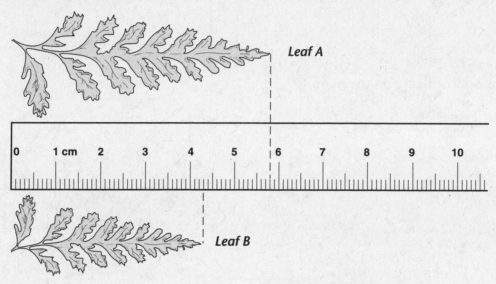

Leaf A

Leaf B

_____ **1.** How many centimeters long is Leaf *A*?

_____ **2.** How many centimeters long is Leaf *B*?

_____ **3.** How many centimeters longer is Leaf *A* than Leaf *B*?

_____ **4.** How many millimeters long is Leaf *A*?

_____ **5.** How many millimeters long is Leaf *B*?

Questions 6–8: Use the diagrams below to answer each question. Write your answer on the line at the left.

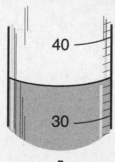
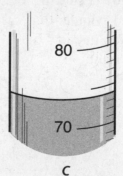

A   **B**   **C**

(Labeled measurements are in mL.)

_____ **6.** What is the volume of the water in graduated cylinder *A*?

_____ **7.** What is the volume of the water in graduated cylinder *B*?

_____ **8.** What is the volume of the water in graduated cylinder *C*?

Skills Test B: Measuring and Calculating *(continued)*

*Questions 9–10: Make the necessary calculations and give
your answer in the space below each question.*

9. What is the area of the rectangle on the right?

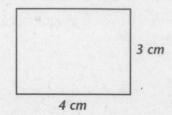

10. What is the volume of the figure on the right?

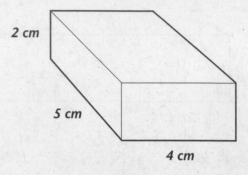

*Questions 11–12: Use the information
provided below and the diagram on
the right to answer the questions. You
can show your work below or use the
back of this page. Write the answer to
each question on the line at the left.*

Suppose you need to measure the
volume of a small rock. You decide to
use water and a graduated cylinder to
find that measurement. You obtain
the results shown on the right.

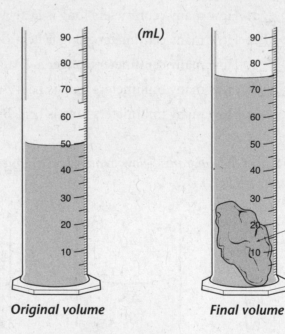

_____11. What is the volume of the water plus the rock?

_____12. What is the volume of the rock alone?

Name _____ Date _____ Class _____

Skills Test B: Measuring and Calculating *(continued)*

Questions 13–14: Use the diagram below to answer each question. Write your answer on the line at the left.

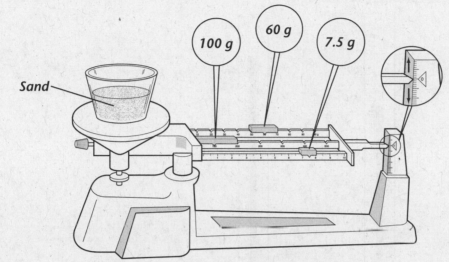

_____ **13.** What is the mass of the container and the sand together?

_____ **14.** If the mass of the container is 14.5 grams, what is the mass of the sand?

Questions 15–19: The diagram below shows five Celsius thermometers. Use these diagrams to answer each question. Write your answer on the line at the left.

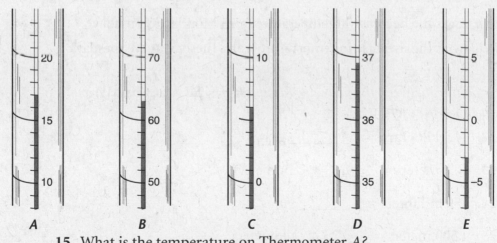

_____ **15.** What is the temperature on Thermometer *A?*

_____ **16.** What is the temperature on Thermometer *B?*

_____ **17.** What is the temperature on Thermometer *C?*

_____ **18.** What is the temperature on Thermometer *D?*

_____ **19.** What is the temperature on Thermometer *E?*

Skills Test B: Measuring and Calculating *(continued)*

Questions 20–21: The diagram below shows a Celsius thermometer on different days.
Use the diagram to answer each question. Write your answer on the line at the left.

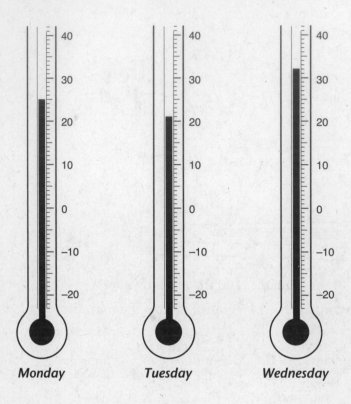

Monday   Tuesday   Wednesday

_____**20.** What was the decrease in temperature from Monday to Tuesday?

_____**21.** What was the increase in temperature from Tuesday to Wednesday?

Questions 22–25: Convert between the following SI units. Show all your work. Write
your answer on the line at the left.

_____ **22.** 34.0 kilograms = _____?_____ grams

_____ **23.** 30.0 meters = _____?_____ centimeters

_____ **24.** 250 milliliters = _____?_____ liters

_____ **25.** 4,500 meters = _____?_____ kilometers

SKILLS ASSESSMENT

Skills Test C: Designing Experiments

Questions 1–10: Match each term in Column 1 with its correct definition from Column 2. Write the letter of the correct answer on the line at the left. Be sure to notice that Column 2 has more definitions than you need to use.

Column 1

_____ **1.** data

_____ **2.** variable

_____ **3.** designing an experiment

_____ **4.** scientific question

_____ **5.** operational definition

_____ **6.** drawing conclusions

_____ **7.** experiment

_____ **8.** interpreting data

_____ **9.** hypothesis

_____ **10.** controlling variables

Column 2

a. any factor that can change in an experiment

b. a careful, orderly test of a hypothesis

c. a statement that describes how a particular variable is to be measured, or how a term is to be defined

d. comparing an object or process to a standard

e. the information gained through observations and measurements

f. keeping all the relevant conditions in an experiment the same except for the manipulated variable

g. a question about the natural world that can be answered by gathering evidence

h. finding meaning in data by looking for patterns or trends

i. making a careful, complete plan for testing a hypothesis

j. making a statement that sums up what you have learned from an experiment

k. using one or more of the five senses to gather information about the world

l. a possible explanation that is tested by an experiment

Skills Test C: Designing Experiments *(continued)*

Questions 11– 20: Column 1 below describes steps that may occur before, during, or after an experiment. Column 2 describes a specific experiment. On the line at the left, write the letter(s) from Column 2 that matches the description in Column 1. Some items from Column 1 may have more than one matching answer from Column 2.

Column 1

_____**11.** conclusion

_____**12.** controlling variables

_____**13.** hypothesis

_____**14.** interpreting data

_____**15.** materials

_____**16.** observations

_____**17.** operational definition

_____**18.** procedure

_____**19.** scientific question(s) that led to the experiment

_____**20.** scientific question(s) that resulted from the experiment

Column 2

A. On a cold winter day, Sayeeda, who lives near a lake, visits her friend Roberto, who lives near the ocean. Sayeeda is surprised to see that the ocean water has no ice on it. The lake near her home is covered with thick ice.

B. Sayeeda asks, "Why doesn't the ocean water have ice on it when the lake does?"

C. Roberto responds, "Well, the lake has fresh water in it. Ocean water contains lots of salt. The salt causes the water to freeze at a lower temperature than usual. I know, because I did an experiment on this in school."

Skills Test C: Designing Experiments *(continued)*

D. Sayeeda says, "I wonder why that happens. Does it just happen with salt? Would the same thing happen with sugar?"

E. Sayeeda and Roberto decide to test this idea, so they write: "If water contains sugar, then it will freeze at a lower temperature than fresh water."

F. They write out these plans:
a. Fill Container *A* and Container *B* with tap water.
b. Dissolve 15 grams of sugar in Container *A*.
c. Place both containers in a freezer kept at −1°C.
d. Leave the containers in the freezer for 24 hours and then observe the contents.

G. They write a list of what they will need: 2 plastic containers, tap water, 15 grams of sugar, 2 wooden stirrers, a freezer.

H. In their notes, they write: "The two containers must be made of the same material and be the same size and shape. The amounts of water must be the same."

I. They decide that if they tilt the container and see any movement in the water, it is not yet frozen. If they tilt it and they observe no change in the water, it is frozen.

J. After 24 hours, Sayeeda and Roberto tilt the containers. They see that the contents of Container *A* flow when they tilt the container. The contents of Container *B* do not move when they tilt the container.

K. They write, "The fresh water froze. The water with sugar dissolved in it did not freeze."

L. They write, "Water that contains sugar freezes at a lower temperature than water without sugar."

M. They then raise these questions: "How cold would it have to get before the water with sugar or salt would freeze? Does it matter how much sugar or salt is in the water? Why does sugar or salt in the water change the way water freezes?"

Skills Test C: Designing Experiments *(continued)*

Questions 21–25: Write the letter of the correct answer on the line at the left.

_____ **21.** Which of the following is an example of a scientific question?
  a. Is experimenting on white mice right or wrong?
  b. Should scientists make as much money as athletes?
  c. Does tanning harm the skin?
  d. Who is the most famous scientist in the world?

_____ **22.** Which of the following is an example of a properly written, testable hypothesis?
  a. People should taste this new health food and see whether it makes them stronger.
  b. When dog owners don't feed their puppies Brand *A* food, the puppies do not grow properly.
  c. If Frederico had added the leaves to the compost pile last year, he wouldn't have to buy organic fertilizer now.
  d. If it is dark, then an owl will find a mouse by the sound the mouse makes.

_____ **23.** Which of the following might be the materials list for an experiment?
  a. data tables and graphs
  b. meters, liters, and kilograms
  c. plastic containers, soil, water, thermometers, and plants
  d. temperature, light, and time

_____ **24.** In an experiment studying the effects of acid rain on pond water, which of the following could be the control?
  a. a container of vinegar to represent the acid
  b. the pond
  c. a container of pond water with nothing added to it
  d. a container of pond water with acid added to it

_____ **25.** In an experiment investigating how far model airplanes with different shapes can travel, which of the following are variables that need to be controlled?
  a. type of wood used; mass of the planes; glue used; air currents and breezes
  b. whether the shapes look like real airplanes; how old the models are
  c. what time the test starts; the time it takes for each test
  d. whether the models land smoothly or become damaged during the test

Name _____ Date _____ Class _____

Skills Test D: Data Tables and Graphs

Questions 1–5: Choose the word or phrase that correctly completes each statement. Write the answer on the line at the left. The same answer may be used more than once.

_____ 1. A graph in which data about separate but related items are represented by rectangular shapes is called a ___?___.

_____ 2. The type of graph that's most useful for showing how one variable changes in response to another variable is called a ___?___.

_____ 3. The type of graph that shows data as parts, or percentages, of a whole is a ___?___.

_____ 4. An organized arrangement of information in labeled rows and columns is called a ___?___.

_____ 5. The type of graph you should use to display data when the manipulated variable is continuous, such as time, temperature, or mass, is a ___?___.

Question 6: Use a separate sheet of paper to make your data table.

6. For a school project, John collected weather data and recorded it in his notebook. Create a data table that organizes the information he collected. Include all the appropriate labeled columns and rows.

September 4, high 28, low 18, partly cloudy
9/5 low 20°C, hi 27, sunny
Sept 6, high 26, low 20, sunny
9/7 high 23, low 19, partly cloudy
9/8 high 29°C, low 21, thunderstorms
Sept 9, low 23, high 28, sunny

Skills Test D: Data Tables and Graphs *(continued)*

Question 7: Use a separate sheet of paper to make your data table.

7. The following is an experiment that Carla and two teammates designed to test how exercise affects heart rate. Create a data table that the lab group could use to record their data. Include a title and labels for the column and rows.

> First, measure my heart rate after I've been sitting still for five minutes. Next walk around the school for five minutes, stop, and measure my heart rate. Last, do jumping jacks for five minutes, stop, and measure heart rate. All heart measurements will be done by taking a pulse for 1 minute immediately after stopping the exercise. Repeat this procedure for the other two people in my lab group, Mike and Una.

Question 8: Use the circle below to make your circle graph.

8. The data table below shows the number of customers who use various energy sources in Pleasantville, a small community of 10,000 homes. Use the circle below to construct a circle graph displaying the data. Label each section of the graph with the energy source and the percent of homes that use it. Make sure you add a title. *(Hint: You can estimate the size of each wedge.)*

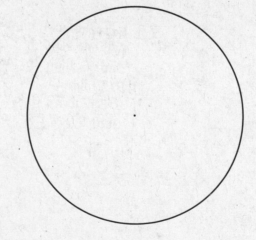

Energy Sources in Pleasantville	
Energy Source	Number of Users
Coal	5,000
Gas	2,500
Solar	1,250
Other	1,250

Inquiry Skills Activity Book I

Skills Test D: Data Tables and Graphs *(continued)*

Question 9: Use the graph paper below to make your graph.

9. The table below shows the different types of waste found in 100 kilograms of a typical family's trash. Use the data to construct a bar graph. Make sure to label the axes and include a title.

Amounts of Different Wastes in 100 kg of Trash	
Type of Waste	**Kilograms**
Paper (newspapers, magazine, packaging, boxes)	34
Yard waste (lawn clippings, leaves)	20
Food	9
Plastics	9
Glass	7
Metal	7
Other (old tires, clothes, rags)	14

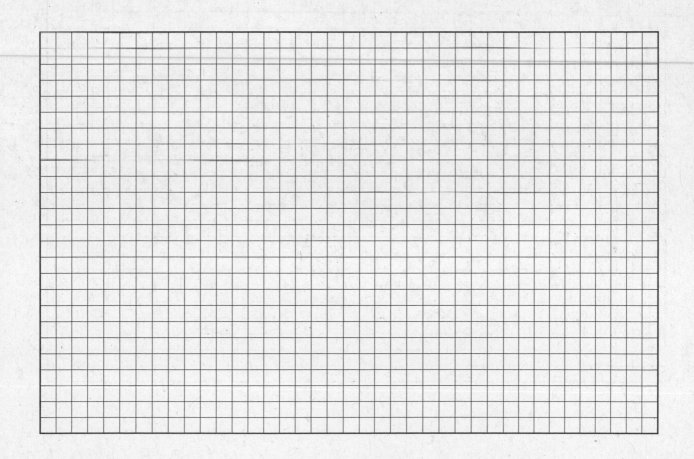

Skills Test D: Data Tables and Graphs *(continued)*

Question 10: Use the graph paper below to make your graph. Write your prediction on the back of this sheet.

10. A scientist was studying the flow of lava from a volcano. Every 30 seconds, she measured how far down the mountain the lava had reached. The data she collected are shown in the data table. Use that information to create a line graph.

Use your line graph to predict when the lava will reach a neighborhood 100 meters away.

Distance of Lava Flow	
Time (min)	**Distance (m)**
0	0
0.5	40
1.0	65
1.5	72
2.0	76
2.5	78
3.0	82
3.5	84
4.0	86
4.5	88
5.0	90

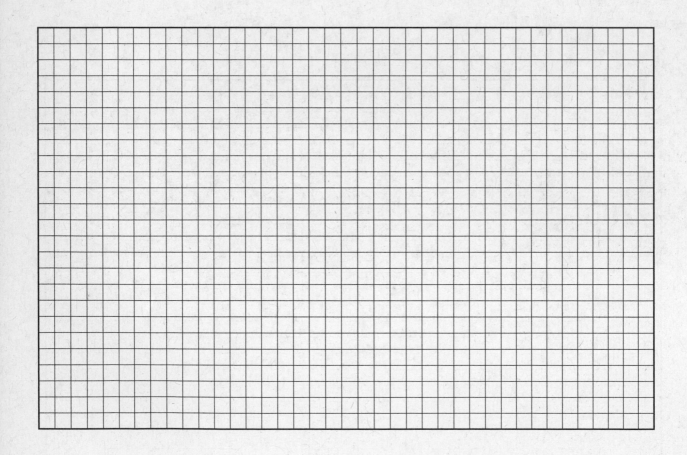

Inquiry Skills Activity Book I

Observing

Introduction (pp. 5–6)

Checkpoint: Answers will vary. Sample: There is ice on the school steps. (qualitative)

Practice (p. 7)

1. Sample: Ground is broken. One house has collapsed. The highway is broken. Some telephone poles are tilted. Some wires are down.

2. Sample: Count the number of trees that are down. Measure the length of the gap in the ground. Measure the horizontal displacement of the two parts of the highway.

3. Answers will vary. Sample inference: An earthquake has occurred.

4. Inference. The illustration does not show the order of events.

5. Inference. The statement relies on cost information not shown in the illustration.

6. Inference. The illustration does not show whether the land is stable or unstable.

7. Inference. The illustration does not show what caused the damage.

8. Answers will vary. Students should include the ideas that an observation is something that you experience directly using your senses, whereas an inference is a possible explanation for an observation.

Inferring

Introduction (pp. 8–9)

Checkpoint: Sample observation—Most of the plants are grasses. Sample inference—The soil conditions allow grasses to grow well.

Practice (pp. 10–11)

1. Animals 1, 2, 4, 5, 7, and 9 have numerous flat teeth. Inference: They probably eat plants.

2. Animals 1, 3, 4, 5, 6, 7, and 8 have numerous sharp teeth. Inference: They probably eat meat.

3. Mammals that eat both plants and animals probably have both sharp teeth and flat teeth. Animals 1, 4, 5, and 7 probably eat both animals and plants.

4. Mammals 3, 4, 5, 6, and 8 appear to have side-by-side eyes. Mammals 1, 2, and 9 appear to have eyes on the sides of their heads.

5. Eyes on the front of the head are advantageous because both eyes can "work together" to help the animal judge how far away a possible prey animal is. However, the animal may not see a prey animal that is too far to the side. Eyes on the sides of the head let an animal see to the side and behind, so that it could see predators creeping up on it. However, it will not be able to judge how far away the predator is.

6. Animal 7. Sample inference: This animal does not depend on its vision to survive, so it may live in the dark, such as underground or in a cave, or be active only at night.

7. Animals 3, 4, 6, and 8 might be hunters.

8. Mammals 2 and 9 might eat plants.

9. Mammals 1, 4, 5, and 7 might eat both plants and animals.

10. Sample: If an extinct animal has teeth that are similar to those of a present-day animal, it is reasonable to infer that the extinct animal ate the same types of food. Similar inferences can be made about the position of the eyes.

Predicting

Introduction (pp. 12–13)

Checkpoint: A science prediction should be based on all the available evidence, including past experience.

Practice (pp. 14–15)

1. Answers will vary based on previous observations or past experience. Samples: Balsa and ebony will float because they are wood. Coal and glass will sink because they're too heavy to float. Sealing wax seems light, so it will probably float.

2. All the cubes that sank had a mass of at least 1.4 g. Those that floated had a mass equal to or less than 0.96 g.

3. Anorthite, coal, diamond, dolomite, and sealing wax will sink; balsa, charcoal, and peat will float. The pattern in Table 1 cannot be used to predict whether tar and ebony will float or sink.

4. Answers will vary. Sample: My predictions for sealing wax are different. I now think sealing wax will sink because the mass of the sealing wax cube is greater than 1.4 g.

5. Sample: The ice cube should have a mass less than 1.4 g.

Classifying

Introduction (p.16)

Checkpoint: Answers will vary. Sample: Clothing worn during the day and clothing worn at night (time of day); subgroups winter and summer clothing (time of year).

Practice (pp. 17–19)

1. Answers will vary. Sample two-group systems: whether or not the animals live in water; whether or not they have legs; whether or not they are domesticated.

2. Answers will vary. Sample: No legs (earthworm, eel, jellyfish, ray, salmon, shark, tuna), 2 legs (bluebird, chicken, duck, goose, hawk, ostrich, robin), 4 legs/flippers (alligator, cow, deer, elephant, frog, monkey, pig, seal, sheep, tiger, tortoise, turtle), 6 legs (fly, grasshopper), 8 legs/tentacles (octopus).

3. Answers will vary. Sample answer: "Lives in water" can be further classified into "lives in fresh water" and "lives in salt water."

4. Answers will vary. Students' classifications should follow the chosen categories.

5. Answers will vary depending on students' answers in Question 1–4. Animals in a zoo could be grouped together according to their habitats, for example, fresh water, salt water, forest, open field, and so on.

6. Answers will vary. Sample: The most useful classifications are based on the animal's habitat or its body structure.

Making Models

Introduction (p. 20)

Checkpoint: Answers will vary. Sample: Physical models of both types look like the objects they represent. Models made for enjoyment may stress surface details, whereas scientific models may stress how things work.

Practice (pp. 21)

1–5. Answers will vary but should be accurate scale models of the classroom.

6–7. Answers will vary but should show an alternate arrangement of the same furniture and equipment as in the current classroom. The explanation of the preferred version should be logical and based on the model.

8. Answers will vary. Sample: I think a physical model has to show the important parts of the object so that you can see how the real object works.

Communicating

Introduction (pp. 23–24)

Checkpoint: Sample—Complete, accurate communication makes it possible to repeat and verify other researchers' experiments.

Practice *(pp. 25–26)*

1. Answers will vary. Sample: What type of container is the best for keeping water hot?

2. Sample: If the container has a vacuum, then it will keep water hot longer.

3. containers with silver layer but no vacuum, with silver layer and vacuum, with no silver layer or vacuum, with vacuum but no silver layer; boiling water, Celsius thermometer, clock

4. Sample: Step 1: Put boiling water into the 4 containers. Step 2: Measure the water temperature in each container. Record the temperatures. Step 3: Repeat Step 2 numerous times after the initial measurement.

5. The table should follow the model given.

6. The graph should be complete, correct, and lead to the following conclusions: The temperature of the water in the silver-lined, vacuum container stayed warmest longest, followed by the other vacuum container, the other silver-lined container, and the container with neither a silver lining nor a vacuum.

7. Sample: The two containers with a vacuum were best at keeping water hot. The container with a vacuum and a silver layer worked best of all.

8. The conclusion supports the hypothesis.

9. Possible questions might include these: How well do the containers keep water hot over longer time periods? Does a larger container keep water hotter than a smaller container with the same construction?

10. Students' summaries should include the main steps of the procedure and results. Using a graph would make it easy to compare the results from the 4 containers.

Measuring

Introduction *(pp. 27–28)*

Checkpoint: Sample—There are 100 cm in a meter and 10 mm in a centimeter. $100 \times 10 = 1,000$, so there are 1,000 mm in a meter.

Practice *(pp. 29–30)*

1. 36 mm		**2.** 3.6 cm	
3. 5 mm		**4.** 0.5 cm	
5. 50 mm		**6.** 5 cm	
7. 7 cm		**8.** 3 cm	
9. 21 cm^2		**10.** 128 cm^3	

11. Yes; a figure 30 mm by 70 mm has the same area as one with 3 cm by 7 cm.

Practice *(p. 31)*

1. 7 mL		**2.** 38 mL
3. 33 mL		**4.** 20 mL
5. 40 mL		

6. Volume of rock: 40 mL   20 mL − 20 mL.

7. Add water to a cylinder; measure the volume. Insert object; measure the volume. Subtract the first volume from the second volume to get the volume of the object.

Practice *(p. 32)*

1. Combined mass: 393.4 g. Mass of substance: 368.4 g (393.4 g − 25 g)

2. 8 g (12 g − 4 g)

3. Each beam shows a different range of masses.

Practice *(p. 33)*

1. 56°C

2. −8°C

3. 73°C

4. 6°C

5. 25°C

6. Question 4: 24 − 18; Question 5: 65 − 40

Calculating

Introduction (pp. 34–35)

Checkpoint: 3,000; 2.082

Practice (p. 36)

1. 0.382
2. 220
3. 450
4. 670
5. 0.303
6. 3,700
7. 4,100
8. 2.11
9. 500,000
10. 1,700

11. Sample: To change 4.5 m to centimeters, multiply by 100 (1 m = 100 cm) by moving the decimal point two places to the right.

Designing Experiments

Introduction (pp. 37–38)

Checkpoint: Sample—Scientists want to test a specific variable and control other variables. If the design is right, they can be confident of the results they obtain.

Posing Questions

Introduction (p. 39)

Checkpoint: The second question is scientific. Sample revision: Does handling toads cause warts?

Practice (p. 40)

Note: Student revisions of scientific questions will vary.

1. Yes; Sample—Will some people be able to perform a specific task, such as adding pairs of numbers, more accurately in the morning, while others perform more accurately in the afternoon?

2. No

3. Yes; Do snakes always travel in pairs?

4. Yes; Do animals, such as pet cats, behave differently just before an earthquake than they do at other times?

5. No

6. No

7. Yes; Do people remember what they read immediately before falling asleep better than what they read earlier in the day?

8. Yes; Can a rider on Maria's kind of bike consistently win a bike race against a rider of equal skill riding Rob's kind of bike?

9. Yes; Do some birds fly to warmer areas every year when temperatures cool in the Fall?

10. Yes; Are the average EPA gas mileage estimates for all trucks lower than those for all cars?

11. Answers will vary. Sample for Question 1: Give people addition quizzes in the morning and afternoon for several days, and compare the two groups of scores.

Developing a Hypothesis

Introduction (p. 41)

Checkpoint: Sample—If a truck carries a load that is equal to 25% of its own weight, it will use more gas than an identical empty truck.

Practice (pp. 42–43)

Note: The story in this activity is based on the fact that the density of drinks with sugar is usually much greater (because there's so much more sugar in the drink) than the density of the same drinks with aspartame.

1. Samples: Maybe the drink has more syrup. Maybe sucrose is heavier than aspartame. Maybe the company puts more bubbles in the diet drink to make it taste better.

2. Samples: Maybe the can that sank is a little larger, or maybe it contains more drink or less air. Maybe one can was damaged.

3. Sample: Maybe the can at the bottom is caught on something.

4. Sample: If you weigh equal volumes of each drink, then the diet drink will weigh less than the regular drink.

5. Sample: If you find the volumes of drink in each can, then there will be less drink in the can that floated.

6. Sample tests: Check the volume of the cans.Weigh the unopened cans, the drinks, or the empty cans. Pour the drinks into graduated cylinders to check their volumes.

7. Sample: List as many different ideas as I can, choose the most sensible one, and then write a hypothesis that can be tested.

Controlling Variables

Introduction (pp. 44–45)

Checkpoint: You can be sure that the manipulated variable is causing the changes in the responding variable only when you control other variables that might affect the outcome.

Practice (p. 46)

All answers are samples.

1. MV: shape of container; RV: time for water to freeze; CV: amount of water, material of containers, initial temperature of water

2. MV: storage temperature; RV: hours of use after storage; CV: use same kind of batteries, same moisture, same expiration date

3. MV: types of fabric; RV: how long fabric can carry heavy load without tearing; CV: initial condition of fabric, size of fabric tested, load used

4. MV: different brands or types of stain remover; RV: how quickly the stain is removed; CV: same type and size of stain, same amount of stain remover applied, how long stain remover is allowed to work

5. If the lab group didn't control essential variables, they can't know what really caused the results of the strength tests. For example, if they used objects of different masses to test strength, maybe one paper towel tore because they used a more massive object.

Forming Operational Definitions

Introduction (p. 47–48)

Checkpoint: Sample—Operational definitions tell researchers how to measure specific variables so that they all do it the same way. If they didn't use the same procedures, they could not check each other's work.

Practice (p. 49)

1. Sample: Use a thermometer to be sure the outdoor temperature is 0°C or below.

2. Sample: Measure the height of each plant daily with a metric ruler. After 3 weeks, the tallest plant is the one that grew fastest.

3. Samples: Order by mass; order by length measured from head to tip of tail.

4. Sample: Better drivers are those who did not cause any accidents and or receive traffic tickets in the past year.

5. Sample: Wet both hands completely, lather all parts of the hands with soap, rinse completely, and repeat once more.

6. Sample: For Question 3, a person could easily arrange animals in a list, starting with animals having the most mass and ending with those with the least mass.

Interpreting Data

Introduction (pp. 50–51)

Checkpoint: Yes. The graph shows that the temperature increases regularly with depth, so you could extend the line on the graph and then make the prediction.

Practice (p. 52)

1. The wolf population declined, while the deer population first increased and then dropped dramatically.

2. 75,000 wolves

3. The wolf population declined significantly.

4. about 15,000 deer

5. The deer population increased sharply to about 100,000 in 1925. Then it dropped to about 18,000 in 1935.

6. Answers will vary. Sample: In 1910, there were about five times as many wolves as deer. In 1917, the sizes of the two populations were about equal.

7. As the wolf population declined, the deer population was able to increase because fewer wolves were killing the deer. Then, there was not enough food for all the deer.

8. Answers will vary. The data are consistent with the idea that wolves are hunters that prey upon deer.

9. Answers will vary, but students should start by examining the title and axis labels before trying to interpret the graphed data.

Drawing Conclusions

Introduction (pp. 53–54)

Checkpoint: Samples—No, because the sunlight is different at different times of the year. Yes, the pattern will be the same, but the temperatures will be lower during other seasons.

Practice (p. 55)

All answers are samples.

1. The black can cooled faster than the white can.

2. Olena's hypothesis was false. The color of the containers does have an effect on the rate at which the cans cool, with black cans cooling faster than white cans.

3. Bruce's hypothesis was supported. Black cans containing hot water cool faster than white cans.

4. Black cans containing hot water cool faster than white cans, but after a period of time, they reach the same temperature.

5. Answers will vary, but students should recognize that both researchers learn more about science either way.

Designing an Experiment

Practice (p. 56)

You may wish to arrange students in small groups to help each other improve on their experiment designs, and then discuss selected designs as a whole class.

1–10. Students should follow all the relevant guidelines in their experimental designs.

11. Answers will vary, but might focus on special equipment that would be needed, or long time periods that might be needed to test some hypotheses.

Creating Data Tables

Introduction (pp. 57–58)

Checkpoint: Sample—If you make places in the data table for every observation you plan to make, an empty box is a reminder that you didn't yet record some data.

Practice (pp. 59–60)

1. The light bulb represents the sun and the pans represent bodies of land and water.

2. MV: the different materials in the pans; RV: temperature of the materials

3. She should control any other variables that might affect her results. Example, the pans must start at the same temperature and be placed away from heaters.

4. The table should include the usual elements, including columns for Time, Light Off or On, Water Temperature, and Soil Temperature.

5. Answers may vary. Students should make sure they include a column indicating whether the light was on or off.

Creating Bar Graphs

Note: Bar graphs can be created with the bars running horizontally or vertically. However, many students have difficulty deciding which axis to use for each variable, so this book introduces only one approach. Once your students are adept at graphing, you may want to allow either type of bar graph.

Introduction (pp. 61–62)

Checkpoint: The number of pets; to show separate but related categories

Practice (p. 63)

1. horizontal axis

2. vertical axis 0–12, with spaces large enough to plot points between whole numbers

3. Titles and labels can be taken from the table.

4. The bars for distance will get longer from left to right.

Creating Line Graphs

Introduction (pp. 64–66)

Checkpoint: With some line graphs, you can infer values you did not measure, so you can make predictions about those values.

Practice (p. 67)

1. The graph should have a horizontal line from 20 minutes to 70 minutes.

2. The graph should show that sometimes the temperature increased and at other times it was constant.

3. The solid melts at 0°C, increases temperature until it boils at 100°C, then increases temperature again after it becomes a gas.

Creating Circle Graphs

Introduction (pp. 68–69)

Checkpoint: In all circle graphs, the wedges should add up to 360° and the percentages should add up to 100%.

Practice (p. 70)

1. The circle graph should follow all the rules.

2. Answers will vary. Sample: About one third of the families surveyed own dogs.

3. Answers will vary. Sample: You may need to round numbers when calculating percents and degrees.

Test A: Basic Process Skills

1. O

2. I

3. O

4. O

5. b

6. a

7. a

8. b

9. b

10. b

11. Answers will vary, but the two groups must fit the definition accurately.

12. Answers will vary, but they must include two correct levels of classification.

13. two

14. scale

15. Yes. With two people sitting on the ends, each of the two people sitting at the corners don't have enough room for their dish, glass, and utensils.

16. Sample: The models helped Marcia make sure that she left enough space for every chair and table setting.

17. About 67 mL

18. 78 mL

19. d

20. a

21. g

22. f

23. b

24. e

25. c

Test B: Measuring and Calculating

1. 5.8 cm

2. 4.3 cm

3. 1.5 cm

4. 58 mm

5. 43 mm

6. 6.2 mL

7. 35 mL

8. 74 mL

9. 12 cm^2

10. 40 cm^3

11. 75 mL

12. 25 mL

13. 167.5 g

14. 153 g

15. 17°C

16. 63°C

17. 6°C

18. 36.9°C

19. −3°C

20. 4°C

21. 11°C

22. 34,000 g

23. 3,000 cm

24. 0.25 L

25. 4.5 km

Test C: Designing Experiments

1. e

2. a

3. i

4. g

5. c

6. j

7. b

8. h

9. l

10. f

11. L

12. H

13. E

14. C, K

15. G

16. A, J

17. I

18. F

19. B, D

20. M

21. c

22. d

23. c

24. c

25. a

Test D: Data Tables and Graphs

1. bar graph

2. line graph

3. circle graph

4. data table

5. line graph

6–7. Creating Data Tables Tables for organizing the data should resemble the ones that follow. (*Note:* Data on p. 83 are presented in an inconsistent manner typical of student notes.)

Weather Conditions for September 4 – September 9			
Date	**High (°C)**	**Low (°C)**	**Conditions**
9/4	28	18	Partly cloudy
9/5	27	20	Sunny
9/6	26	20	Sunny
9/7	23	19	Partly cloudy
9/8	29	21	Thunder-storms
9/9	28	23	Sunny

Heart Rate vs. Exercise			
	Heart Rates (beats per minute)		
Person	**Sitting**	**Walking**	**Jumping Jacks**
Carla			
Mike			
Una			

Partial credit could be given as follows:

(**6 points**) Using the manipulated and responding variables for column and/or row heads.

(**2 points**) Using appropriate units in heads.

(**2 points**) Giving the table an appropriate title.

8. Creating Circle Graphs The completed circle graph should resemble the one below.

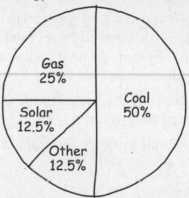

Energy Sources in Pleasantville

Partial credit could be given as follows:

(**6 points**) Calculating the correct number of degrees in each wedge.

(**6 points**) Estimating and drawing the wedges on the circle template.

(**6 points**) Converting numbers into correct percents.

(**1 point**) Label each wedge with the correct category.

(**1 point**) Using an appropriate title.

9. Creating Bar Graphs The completed bar graph should resemble the one below.

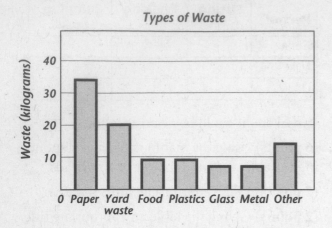

Partial credit could be given as follows:

(**4 points**) Drawing horizontal and vertical axes.

(**5 points**) Choosing and labeling categories for each axis.

(**5 points**) Determining an appropriate, uniform scale, such that all values can be represented on the graph and that each square has the same value.

(**5 points**) Labeling the amount scale at regular intervals along one axis.

(**1 point**) Writing a title for the graph.

10. Creating Line Graphs The completed line graph should resemble the one at the bottom of the page.

Partial credit could be given as follows:

(**2 points**) Drawing horizontal and vertical axes.

(**3 points**) Labeling the horizontal, or x, axis with the name of the manipulated variable and labeling the vertical, or y, axis with the name of the responding variable.

(**3 points**) Creating scales for the graph such that the scales cover the entire range of the data collected for each variable.

(**2 points**) Marking off equally spaced intervals along each axis.

(**2 points**) Labeling each scale such that each begins with 0 or a number that is slightly less than the smallest number to be graphed.

(**3 points**) Correctly plotting each point.

(**1 point**) Connecting the plotted points.

(**1 point**) Giving the graph an appropriate title.

(**3 points**) Extrapolating from the graph that the lava will reach the neighborhood in about 8 minutes.

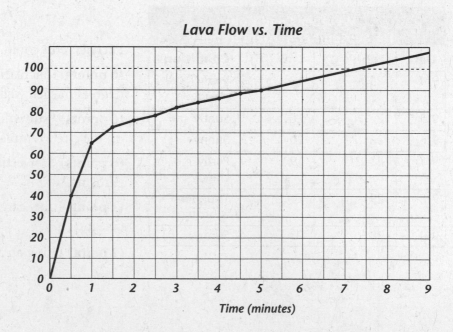